D1536846

AMERICANS
WITH
DISABILITIES
ACT
FACILITIES
COMPLIANCE

AMERICANS
WITH
DISABILITIES
ACT
FACILITIES
COMPLIANCE

A
Practical
Guide

Evan Terry Associates, PC

Birmingham, Alabama

John Wiley & Sons, Inc.
New York • Chichester • Brisbane • Toronto • Singapore

Library of Congress Cataloging in Publication Data:
Americans with Disabilities Act facilities compliance : a practical
    guide / Evan Terry Associates, P.C.
        p.   cm.
        Includes index.
        ISBN 0-471-59192-0 (paper)
        1. Architecture and the physically handicapped––Law and
    legislation––United States.   I. Evan Terry Associates, P.C.
    KF5709.3.H35A96   1993
    343.73'07872'042––dc20
    [347.3037872042]   92-32832

Printed in United States of America

10 9 8 7 6 5 4 3

20.42
ne

Introduction

ADA History

What is ADA?

Issues of Title II and Title III

Accessibility Guidelines

Table of Contents

Introduction

Preface

This reference manual is meant as a tool to help you understand the facilities requirements of the ADA, as well as offering you compliance strategies. It would be a good bet that at this moment you're wondering how ADA will affect you and the facilities associated with your organization. We at Evan Terry Associates were faced with answering that very same question July 26, 1990, the day that the Americans with Disabilities Act was signed into Law by President Bush. To answer this question for our clients we had to thoroughly research the Law, proposed and final regulations, pertinent accessibility standards and the available Congressional Hearing Reports on ADA. After researching this Law we recognized that the facility compliance requirements of the Law are only part of the "big picture". The other parts consist of employment related issues as well as transportation, customer services and communications. The employment issues are addressed by employment law specialists and we will leave the details of these as well as transportation, communication and customer service issues to those more qualified to address those issues. Our focus will be on the facilities issues of ADA.

As architects and accessible design specialists, we think our energies are best utilized by writing this book from the perspective of an architect or client rather than an attorney. You will need to consult your attorney for specific applications of the ADA for your organization.

We begin with the history and background of ADA. Next, we review the five Titles (or parts) associated with this Law, effective dates, regulations, enforcement, exemptions and tax benefits. Also included under the second section, "What is ADA?", are the Compliance Fact Sheets, Time Table and Flow Chart that help you to understand the process associated with facilities compliance. The next section is "Title II and Title III Issues" and we address the legal issues associated with facilities operated and/or owned by state or local governmental agencies (Title II) and issues associated with privately owned and/or operated facilities (Title III). Next, we include an overview of the technical specifications titled "Accessibility Guidelines". It is here that we identify elements along the exterior accessible route and interior accessible route that are considered barriers for individuals with disabilities. Also in this section, we address special occupancy concerns for those who have restaurants, healthcare facilities, retail spaces, libraries or transient lodging facilities. Lastly, we summarize the facilities issues under the section titled "Compliance Strategies."

It is also important for you to know that the Fact Sheets which summarize the requirements of the Law, the Facilities Compliance Flow Chart and Time Table mentioned above, can be utilized as a "short form" reminder of the major issues covered by ADA or as an executive summary to assist you in communicating basic ADA facility compliance requirements to others in your organization.

Before we get into the heart of the issues of ADA Facilities Compliance, we need to reinforce to you that this document is to be used in conjunction with the ADA Accessibility Guidelines (ADAAG) and the latest Federal regulations associated with Title II and Title III of this Act, which were published in the FEDERAL REGISTER (28 CFR Parts 35 & 36) on July 26, 1991. This book is not intended to be a substitute for the ADAAG, nor the federal regulations, nor any other applicable state or local accessibility code. It is intended that you use it to gain a better over-all understanding of the facility compliance issues of the ADA. Best of luck to you.

Bill Hecker, AIA, Editor
Accessible Design Specialist
EVAN TERRY ASSOCIATES, P.C.

Acknowledgements

We especially appreciate the guidance and technical assistance we received during our preparation of the ADA Facilities Compliance program from the man who literally "wrote the book" on accessible design in the United States, Mr. Ronald L. Mace, FAIA. He and his associates at Barrier Free Environments, Inc., especially Jim Bostrom and Leslie Young, provided valuable comments and suggestions regarding the contents of this publication.

In addition to the two principals, James L. Terry, AIA, and Malcolm L. Sokol, AIA, who supported this project from the beginning, the following staff members at Evan Terry Associates, P. C. should also be acknowledged: in particular, the typing efforts of Christa Buchanan and Diane Booker; the computer publishing efforts of Don Bolin, AIA, George Sporl, ASLA, and Eugene Edgerly; for their efforts associated with the preparation of the "survey forms included in the full workbook,"

Marvin Martin, FCSI, Dave Snider, AIA, Frank Carra, and
Meng Lee; for the technical insights of Neil H. King, Jr., AIA,
Gary W. Justiss, AIA, and Gene S. Jones, AIA; the management
skills of Harriet Ingram; and last but not least, the "glue" that
held this whole process together, Sandra Cox. We must also
acknowledge the graphic design assistance and dependable com-
puterized layout services of Strategic Solutions of Birmingham,
Alabama.

*   *   *

ADA History

*Today, we're here to rejoice in and celebrate
"Independence Day", one that is long overdue. With
today's signing of the landmark Americans with Disabilities Act, every man, woman and child with a
disability can now pass through once closed doors into
a bright new era of equality, independence and freedom.*

With those words President Bush signed into law the Americans
with Disabilities Act (ADA) at 10:26 AM Eastern Daylight
Time, July 26, 1990. Doing so, the United States was thrust into
the forefront of world concern for people with disabilities. Never
before in any country in the world has there been such a
comprehensive civil rights law to ensure the equality of people
with disabilities.

Justin Dart, the 1990 Chairman of the President's Committee on
Employment of People with Disabilities clearly outlined the
reasons behind the passage of ADA in his article in the fall 1990
ADA Special Issue of "Work Life" magazine:

> With the development of modern medicine and social
> responsibility millions of 20th century humans are
> surviving previously fatal conditions and living on
> with significant disabilities. These individuals have a
> great potential to be happy, productive members of
> our communities. However, our best efforts to fulfill
> this potential have been consistently limited by a
> massive residue of prejudice and paternalism. Our
> society is still infected by an insidious, now almost
> subconscious assumption that people with disabilities
> are less than fully human, and therefore are not fully
> eligible for the opportunities, services and support
> systems which are available to other people as a
> matter of right.

> More than two decades ago many of us in the disabil-
> ity community concluded that Americans with disabil-
> ities would never achieve full, productive citizenship
> until this nation made a firm statement of law pro-
> tecting their civil right.

> The Americans with Disabilities Act is such a law. It
> establishes "a clear and comprehensive prohibition of
> discrimination on the basis of disability." Taken in
> combination with previously existing disability rights

law, it provides a sound legal framework for the practical implementation of the inalienable right of all people with disabilities to participate in the mainstream of society. It extends to people with disabilities the same protection of their right that is already enjoyed by the members of all other minorities.

In the quote above Justin Dart mentioned a few of the factors, such as developments in modern medicine and social responsibility, that have played a part in why ADA is here and here to stay. Many individuals, including Justin Dart, have for years played key roles in the disability rights movement in America. Several factors have played a part in making the disability rights community as strong as it is today. Among these factors are the lobbying efforts of disabled veterans, who after sacrificing for our country returned to find that the opportunities that were available to them before being disabled were now unavailable to them as disabled Americans. These veterans played an important part in lobbying Congress for much of the legislation that protects people with disabilities. Another group instrumental in pushing this issue was the group of individuals affected by polio epidemics in the forty's and fifty's. Other factors include increasing medical technological innovations used to save the lives of those who in the past would have died. These medical innovations along with the "graying" of America contribute to a growing population of people with disabilities. The "graying" of America can be attributed in part to a shift in the demographic "bubble" of the baby boom as those born in the forties, fifties and sixties move into their senior years. The benefits from the facility compliance provisions of ADA will also help this group. In addition to these factors there has been a marked shift from the institutionalization of people with disabilities to homecare and an independent lifestyle.

After reviewing the factors mentioned above, we can begin to understand why ADA came about but we really can't understand it's history unless we look at previous federal legislation dealing with accessibility. Before ADA you could very easily categorize federal legislation into "facilities accessibility" legislation and "program accessibility" legislation.

A major milestone in the history of barrier free design was the development of the American National Standards Institute (ANSI) document A117.1 entitled "American National Standard Specifications for Making Building and Facilities Accessible to and Useable by the Physically Handicapped". This short publication, only a few pages long, was the culmination of the first barrier free design research in America. It was conducted under a grant from the Easter Seal Research Foundation by the University of Illinois. Later the National Easter Seal Society along with the President's Committee on Employment of the Handicapped, were designated as the Secretariat of this endeavor. This document has been revised and expanded many times since 1961 and is currently used as a reference standard by many states and local governments in their laws which mandate accessibility.

With the ANSI A117.1 Standards being adopted by many state and municipal governments, the federal government passed a law in 1969 called the Architectural Barriers Act. The ABA essentially states that if federal dollars are earmarked for the construction of a facility, that facility must be designed to be accessible to and useable by persons with disabilities. The standard for construction here is not the ANSI A117.1 Standard but rather the Uniform Federal Accessibility Standards (UFAS). The UFAS standards are built upon the 1980 version of the ANSI A117.1. This ABA legislation typifies "facility accessibility" legislation put forth by the federal government.

The other type of legislation introduced or adopted by the federal government is "program accessibility" legislation. The most important program accessibility legislation before the ADA was the Rehabilitation Act of 1973. Section 504 of the Rehab Act and subsequent modifications to that act state, essentially, if an organization receives federal financial assistance through grants, loans or other means, all programs offered by that organization must be made accessible to people with disabilities when the programs are viewed in their entirety.

As you can see, all this federal legislation is dependant upon some form of federal dollars trickling down to a particular organization. The same could be held true for most state and municipal disability rights laws, but the ADA fills in the "cracks" where state and federal laws do not cover programs or facilities. ADA covers all types of companies and agencies, with few exceptions, regardless of whether they receive tax dollars. That is the big difference between ADA and other existing laws and that is why President Bush in his signing speech stated the following:

> Last year, we celebrated a victory of international freedom. Even the strongest person couldn't scale the Berlin Wall to gain the elusive promise of independence that lay just beyond and so together we rejoiced when that barrier fell.

> And now I sign legislation which takes a sledgehammer to another wall, one which has ...for too many generations separated Americans with Disabilities from the freedom they could glimpse but could

not grasp. Once again we rejoice as this barrier falls proclaiming together we will not accept, we will not excuse, we will not tolerate discrimination in America...Let the shameful wall of exclusion finally come tumbling down.

Therefore, what began as a recommendation from the National Council on Disabilities after their 1986 study called "Toward Independence", and transcended Congressional debate and Committee hearings, was made the law of the land.

*   *   *

What is ADA?

Introduction

For most of you reading this workbook, assuming you are associated with your organization's facilities in some way, the issues of Title II and Title III will, almost certainly, be your primary concern. The first step in learning the facility compliance requirements of ADA is to identify what type of organization you represent. Your options are simple—either a public entity or a private entity. The requirements are very different depending on your status.

In case you are wondering what type you are, a public entity is one that is associated with a state or local governmental agency, board or other subset. A private entity is everyone else except for federal agencies and specifically exempt entities. Before you read any further, identify your organization as either a public entity or a private entity—then burn that designation into your memory. It will be the basis for what you will have to do to comply with ADA.

For those of you representing public entities, you will need to watch for the requirements of Title II. For you who represent private entities, watch for the requirements of Title III. I cannot reinforce strongly enough how important it will be for you to know what type of organization you represent. With that behind us, let's learn how this law came about.

Anti-Discrimination Law

On July 26, 1990 President Bush signed the Americans with Disabilities Act of 1990. The White House touted it as being "the broadest expansion of the nation's civil rights law since the Civil Rights Act of 1964". This legislation expands the network of federal civil rights laws currently applying to women and minorities to include the 43 million Americans with some form of disability and was said to "allow an unprecedented opportunity to bring Americans with disabilities into the mainstream of American life". This act began in 1986 with Vice President Bush accepting a report entitled "Toward Independence" from the National Council on Disabilities which contained broad legislation expanding federal civil rights laws to include persons with disabilities. In the 1988 campaign, Vice President Bush again supported the legislation to extend the same basic equal

 **ADA Facilities Compliance**™
7-92

opportunity protections afforded women and minorities to persons with disabilities. In his February 9, 1989 address to congress entitled "Building a Better America", the President said, "disabled Americans must become full partners in America's opportunity society". It is interesting to note that ADA passed the Senate by a vote of 91 to 6 and the House by a vote of 377 to 28. What follows is a summary of the five Titles of ADA:

Title I	ADA Employment Section
Title II	ADA Public Services and Public Transportation Section (Public Entities)
Title III	ADA Public Accommodations and Services Section (Private Entities)
Title IV	ADA Telecommunications Section
Title V	ADA Miscellaneous Provisions

Effective Dates—Title II

After January 26, 1992 public entities that are not in compliance with the general requirements of Title II as well as the program accessibility requirements and alteration/new construction requirements are at risk of complaint or civil law suit. The following list of dates will be of assistance in understanding when each compliance requirement is to be addressed:

1-26-1992

1. Ensure that the operation of each service, program and activity is operating so that each, when viewed in its entirety, is readily accessible to and usable by individuals with disabilities. (35.150(a))

   Even though the following required procedures will not shield a public entity from a discrimination complaint, they are mandatory if programs are not readily accessible to and usable by people with disabilities.

   A. Begin **self-evaluation** process for those areas of services, policies and practices not previously evaluated (and on file) for section 504 of the Rehabilitation Act of 1973. (35.105)

   B. Public entities with 50 or more employees begin **transition plan** outlining structural changes selected for program accessibility and proceed with structural changes, as required, to facilities "as expeditiously as possible". (35.150(c))

2. New construction starting after this date must be readily accessible. (35.151(a))

3. The altered portions of alterations advertised for bid after this date must, to the maximum extent feasible, meet the "readily accessible to and usable by individuals with disabilities" standard set by the Uniform Federal Accessibility Standard or, at the public entity's option, the ADAAG. (35.151(b))

4. Date a complaint or civil law suit may be filed by an individual based on ADA discrimination by a public entity.

7-26-1992

Transition plan complete where structural changes to facilities will be undertaken to provide program access. Transition plan must identify obstacles, describe in detail the methods that will be used to make facilities accessible, specify the schedule for taking the steps identified and indicate the official responsible for implementation of the plan. (35.150(d))

1-26-1993

Self-evaluation complete. (35.105(a))

1-26-1995

Completion of last structural changes to facilities where such changes were undertaken for program accessibility. (35.150(c))

Effective Dates—Title III

Barrier Removal:

With regard to civil actions taken against public accommodation entities that have discriminated against people with disabilities by not removing barriers from facilities where such removal was readily achievable, the effective date is 1-26-1992. Congress has seen fit to extend the civil suit initiation date for **smaller businesses.** The suit initiation date for those businesses that employ 25 people or fewer and have gross receipts of $1,000,000 or less shall be **July 26, 1992.** For those companies or businesses that employ 10 or fewer employees and have gross receipts of $500,000 or less, the effective date shall be **January 26, 1993.**

Alterations:

Although the legal language of Section 310 that stipulates the effective dates of each element of Title III is rather ambiguous as to the actual effective date for those suits brought against entities that discriminate by construction of alterations under Section 303, the ATBCB and the Department of Justice have confirmed that the compliance date for this portion of Title III shall be January 26, 1992. Alteration work starting after that date must meet the ADAAG.

New Construction:

For those new construction projects whose first occupancy is after January 26, 1993, the requirements of Section 303 shall apply.

The Department of Justice has defined that a facility is "designed and constructed for first occupancy after January 26, 1993" if .....

> (A) the last application for a building permit (or permit extension) is received and certified complete by the governmental agency having authority, after January 26, 1992; and,
> (B) the first certificate of occupancy is issued after January 26, 1993.

It is important to understand that the definition above states the "last" application for permit. This means, if you apply for a "foundation permit" before the 1-26-92 deadline but don't apply for the "super structure" permit until after that date, the super structure must be designed to be fully accessible (if Certificate of Occupancy is issued after 1-26-93).

Regulations

The **United States Attorney General** was required to issue regulations associated with the requirements of the ADA not later than one year after enactment or July 26, 1991.

The Coordination and Review Section, Civil Rights Division of the U.S. Department of Justice was responsible for coordinating the development of these regulations. The regulations from the Department of Justice include those required standards from the Architectural Transportation Barrier Compliance Board (ATBCB) as Appendix A.

The ATBCB provided supplemental guidelines (ADA Accessibility Guidelines for Buildings and Facilities) to the Minimum Guidelines and Regulations Requirements for Accessible Design (MGRAD). MGRAD is the basis on which the Uniform Federal Accessibility Standards (UFAS) were formulated and UFAS

Standards were utilized as the "interim accessibility standard" for projects wishing to be in compliance with ADA before the final ADA Accessibility Guidelines (ADAAG) were published.

Enforcement of ADA—Title II

Individuals who believe themselves to be discriminated against may follow one of two options: either file a complaint with a Federal agency having jurisdiction or file a civil lawsuit in Federal District Court. The law states that enforcement remedies, procedures and rights set out in Section 505 of the Rehabilitation Act of 1973 (including by reference Remedies of Civil Rights Act - 1964) are the same as those set forth for Title II ADA enforcement.

An individual who believes that he or she has been discriminated against on the basis of their disability by a public entity may file a complaint with the appropriate federal agency under whose jurisdiction the alleged discriminating program lies. This complaint must be filed no later than 180 days from the date of the alleged discrimination. The designated agency shall then investigate the complaint to attempt an "informal resolution", and if a resolution is not achieved, then that agency may issue a "Letter of Findings" which includes the following:

1. Findings of fact and conclusions of the law;

2. A description of a remedy for each violation found; and

3. Notice of the rights available under this section including the right for a complainant to file a private lawsuit.

The "Letter of Findings" is then forwarded to the Assistant U.S. Attorney General. The designated agency then must initiate negotiations with the public entity in an attempt to secure compliance by voluntary means. If the agency cannot negotiate compliance on a voluntary basis, then the matter will be forwarded to the U. S. Attorney General for appropriate action. For lists of appropriate federal agencies refer to the regulations for Title II published in the Federal Register on Friday, July 26, 1991 (35.190).

At any time in the enforcement process, a complainant may elect to file a private civil suit in the Federal Court having the appropriate jurisdiction.

Because the administrative enforcement procedure is the same as the Rehabilitation Act, the remedies of this Act make "the sanction of 'fund termination' available where necessary to achieve compliance" as stated in the Title II regulations preamble. "Fund termination" is available for only the violations of Section 504, not for all Title II requirements, and only for programs receiving federal financial assistance.

The federal agencies designated under ADA to assist and process complaints of Title II discrimination include the following for the activities and programs described:

(1) Department of Agriculture: All programs, services and regulatory activities relating to farming and the raising of livestock, including extension services.

(2) Department of Education: All programs, services, and regulatory activities relating to the operation of elementary and secondary education systems and institutions, institutions of higher education and vocational education (other than schools of medicine, dentistry, nursing, and other health-related schools), and libraries.

(3) Department of Health and Human Services: All programs, services, and regulatory activities relating to the provision of health care and social services, including schools of medicine, dentistry, nursing, and other health related schools, the operation of healthcare and social service providers and institutions, including "grass-roots" and community services organizations and programs, and preschool and daycare programs.

(4) Department of Housing and Urban Development: All programs, services, and regulatory activities relating to state and local public housing, and housing assistance and referral.

(5) Department of Interior: All programs, services, and regulatory activities relating to lands and natural resources, including parks and recreation, water and waste management, environmental protection, energy, historic and cultural preservation, and museums.

(6) Department of Justice: All programs, services, and regulatory activities relating to law enforcement, public safety, and the administration of justice, including courts and correctional institutions; commerce and industry, including general economic development, banking and finance, consumer protection, insurance, and small business; planning, development, and regulations (unless assigned to other designated agencies); state and local government support services (e.g.,

audit, personnel, comptroller, administrative services); all other government functions not assigned to other designated agencies.

(7) Department of Labor: All programs, services, and regulatory activities relating to labor and the work force.

(8) Department of Transportation: All programs, services, and regulatory activities relating to transportation, including highways, public transportation, traffic management (non-law enforcement), automobile licensing and inspection, and driver licensing.

Enforcement of ADA—Title III

Section 308 of the law establishes enforcement options for those being discriminated against by a private entity on the basis of a disability and in violation of Title III. The same remedies and procedures as are found in Section 204 (a) of the **Civil Rights Act of 1964** (including the option for court-appointed, no-cost attorneys for compliance) shall apply to the enforcement of ADA therefore tying discrimination against people with disabilities to the civil rights of the past.

The law states that discrimination legal procedures can be initiated by anyone who is being subjected to discrimination on the basis of one or more disabilities or who has **"reasonable grounds for believing"** that they are **about to be** subjected to discrimination in violation of a condition in Section 303 (which refers to new construction and alterations to public accommodations and commercial facilities). The proposed regulations on Title III stated the following with regard to what might be called a "preemptive strike" using the "reasonable grounds" concept mentioned above:

> Authorizing suits to prevent construction of facilities with architectural barriers will avoid the necessity of costly retrofitting that might be required if suits were not permitted until after the facilities were completed.

The law continues by stating that "nothing in this Section shall require a person with a disability to engage in a **futile gesture** if such person has actual notice that a person or organization covered by this Title does not intend to comply with its provision".

It is interesting to note that these remedies and procedures set forth under Section 204 (A) of the Civil Rights Act of 1964, in general, include injunctive relief, that is an application for a permanent or temporary restraining order or other order. With regard to the **readily achievable removal of architectural barriers** noted under Section 302 and the **new construction and alterations** provisions under Section 303, violation of these provisions allows for **injunctive relief** which includes an order to make them **readily accessible to and usable by** individuals with disabilities "to the extent required by this Title". The law also goes on to state "appropriate injunctive relief shall also include requiring the provisions of an **auxiliary aid or service, modification** of the policy, or provision of **alternative methods,** to the extent required by this Title".

The U.S. Attorney General shall be responsible for investigating alleged violations of Title III and shall "undertake periodic reviews of compliance of covered entities under this Title". The preamble states the following with regard to the Attorney General's enforcement role:

> Although the Act does not establish a comprehensive administrative enforcement mechanism for investigation and resolution of all complaints received, the legislative history notes that investigation of alleged violations and periodic compliance reviews are essential to effective enforcement of title III, and that the Attorney General is expected to engage in active enforcement and to allocate sufficient resources to carry out this responsibility.

The law states for Title III that if the Attorney General has "reasonable cause to believe" that someone is engaged in "**a pattern or practice of discrimination** under this Title" or if someone has been discriminated against under this Title, and that discrimination raises **"an issue of general public importance"** then the Attorney General may file civil action in any United States district court. Again, quoting from Congressional Reports, the authority of the court with regard to civil action by the Attorney General as noted above can include the following:

> (The Court) may grant any **equitable relief** that such court considered to be appropriate, including to the extent required by this Title 1.) granting temporary, preliminary or permanent relief, 2.) providing an auxiliary aid or service, modification of policy, practice, or procedure, or alternative methods, and 3.) making facilities readily accessible to and usable by individuals with disabilities. The court may also

award such other relief as it considers "to be appropriate, including **monetary damages** to persons aggrieved when requested by the Attorney General" and the court may also "vindicate the public interest" by assessing a "**civil penalty** against the entity in the amount not to exceed **$50,000** for the first violation and not to exceed **$100,000** for any subsequent violation".

The law states that **punitive damages** are not available but **"monetary damages"** and "such other relief" are available. The House Report reflects upon this particular issue as follows:

Section 308(b)(4) clarifies that the term 'monetary damages' and 'other relief' in Section 308(b)(2) does **not** include **punitive damages.** It does include however, all forms of compensatory damages, including out of pocket expenses and damages for pain and suffering. The Attorney General has discretion regarding the type of damages he or she seeks on behalf of the aggrieved person if he or she chooses to seek such monetary damages.

It is also important to note that **attorney's fees,** including litigation expenses, and costs are part of the damages a prevailing party may be awarded, if the court desires. The U.S. Government is also liable for these potential damages under Section 505.

With regard to **judicial consideration,** the law states that civil action pertaining to violations that show a pattern or practice of discrimination and/or those that seem to be an issue of general public importance, should be given consideration by the court with regard to any **"good faith effort"** or "attempt to comply with this act" by the entity. Regarding the meaning of "good faith" the law states "the court shall consider among other factors it deems relevant, whether the entity could have reasonably anticipated the need for an appropriate type of auxiliary aid needed to accommodate the unique needs of a particular individual with a disability". The "good faith" standard should be conscientiously enacted to help protect your organization from the assessment of civil penalties. Those entities that have honestly and reasonably attempted to comply with the law will probably lessen their risk of being assessed civil penalties. Congressional reports elaborate as follows:

For example, a public accommodation is not required to anticipate all the auxiliary aids that might be necessary to accommodate an individual with a **unique disability.** While of course, a public accommodation is expected to anticipate such disabilities as **visual, speech, hearing and mobility impairments.** The Committee does not, as reflected in the statutory language, expect that the civil penalties will be assessed against entities that reasonably and honestly could not have anticipated the unique needs of individuals with certain types of unusual disabilities and therefore may not have had some appropriate auxiliary aid at hand. Of course, once an individual has been identified and requested a specific auxiliary aid, the public accommodation cannot subsequently claim that the aid could not have been reasonably anticipated. The public accommodation, of course, would not have to provide the aid if it would impose an **undue burden.** In sum, an honest effort to comply with the law should be a basic factor taken into account by the court in assessing whether any civil penalties or the highest level of those penalties should apply against a public accommodation.

The Attorney General is also given authority to "**certify** that a state law or local building code or similar ordinance that establishes accessibility requirements meets or exceeds the minimum requirements of this act for the accessibility and useability of covered facilities under this Title". The Attorney General must also consult with the **Architectural and Transportation Barriers Compliance Board** and have a public hearing to review the issue of certification of local accessibility standards as equivalent to those required under ADA. The Congressional Reports offer some suggestions for this particular responsibility of the Attorney General:

> This provision is intended simply to allow builders and architects to use codes and laws with which they are familiar, if those laws, in fact, meet or exceed the requirements of this act. This provision is not intended in any way to allow entities to avoid the purposes and goals of this act. Thus, the Committee expects that the Attorney General will carefully scrutinize any such requests for certification and seriously consider any objections raised by individuals with disabilities to such certification, if such objections are made.

Alternative Means of Dispute Resolution

The law states that where appropriate and "to the extent authorized by the law, the use of **alternative means of dispute resolution,** including settlement negotiations, conciliation, facilitation, mediation, fact finding, mini-trials, and arbitration is encouraged to resolve disputes arising under this Act".

Exemptions from Title III

The law exempts **private clubs** or establishments, **religious organizations,** entities controlled by religious organizations, and those establishments exempted from coverage under Title II of the **Civil Rights Act of 1964** from the provisions of Title III of this act.

Regarding **religious organizations** and entities controlled by religious organizations, the preamble to the Title III regulations say the following:

> The ADA's exemption of religious organizations and religious entities controlled by religious organizations is very broad, encompassing a wide variety of situations. Religious organizations and entities controlled by religious organizations have no obligations under the ADA. Even when a religious organization carries out activities that would otherwise make it a public accommodation, the religious organization is exempt from ADA coverage. Thus, if a church itself operates a day care center, a nursing home, a private school, or a diocesan school system, the operations of the center, home, school, or schools would not be subject to the requirements of the ADA or this part. The religious entity would not lose its exemption merely because the services provided were open to the general public. The test is whether the church or other religious organization operates the public accommodation, not which individuals receive the public accommodation's services.

Along with the above mentioned entities that are exempt from Title III, there are two other building types that do not have to comply to the ADA. Residential projects, either single-family or multi-family are not covered by ADA. Multi-family projects are required to meet the accessibility requirements of the Fair Housing Amendments Act of 1988. Federal building projects are not covered by ADA because, since 1968 these facilities have had to meet the accessibility requirements of the Architectural Barriers Act.

Tax Credits and Deductions

The Internal Revenue Code, as amended in 1990, will allow a deduction of up to $15,000 per year for costs associated with the removal of qualified architectural and transportation barriers. The amendment of 1990 also allows certain small business (those with gross receipts of less than $1,000,000 or those with 30 or fewer full-time workers) to claim a tax credit of up to 50% of eligible access expenditures in excess of $250 but not more than $10,250. The regulations from the Department of Justice state that eligible access expenditures include "necessary and reasonable costs of removing barriers, providing auxiliary aids, and acquiring or modifying equipment or devices".

* * *

ADA Facilities Compliance Program
A Guide to Understanding the Americans with Disabilities Act

Definitions

Disability - (a) A physical or mental impairment that substantially limits one or more of the major life activities of an individual; (b) A record of such impairment; or (c) Being regarded as having an impairment.

Facility - all or any portion of buildings, structures, sites, complexes, rolling stock or other conveyances, equipment, roads, walks, passageways, parking lots, or other real or personal property, including the site where the building, property, structure, or equipment is located. Includes both indoor and outdoor areas where human-constructed improvements, structures, equipment or property has been added to the natural environment.

Place of Public Accommodation - a facility operated by a private entity falling within at least one of these 12 categories: (a) an inn, hotel, motel, or other place of lodging except for an establishment located within a building that contains not more than five rooms for rent or hire and that is actually occupied by the proprietor of such establishment as the residence of such proprietor; (b) a restaurant, bar or other establishment serving food or drink; (c) a motion picture house, theater, concert hall, stadium or other place of exhibition or entertainment; (d) an auditorium, convention center, lecture hall or other place of public gathering; (e) a bakery, grocery store, clothing store, hardware store, shopping center or other sales or rental establishment; (f) a laundromat, dry cleaner, bank, barber shop, beauty shop, travel service, shoe repair service, funeral parlor, gas station, office of an accountant or lawyer, pharmacy, insurance office, professional office of a healthcare provider, hospital, or other service establishment; (g) a terminal depot or other station used for specified public transportation; (h) a museum, library, gallery, or other place of public display or collection; (i) a park, zoo, amusement park or other place of recreation; (j) a nursery, elementary, secondary, undergraduate, or post graduate private school or other place of education; (k) a day care center, senior citizens center, homeless shelter, food bank, adoption agency or other social service center establishment; (l) a gymnasium, health spa, bowling alley, golf course or other place of exercise or recreation.

Commercial Facilities - facilities that are intended for non-residential use by a private entity whose operations will affect commerce.

Readily Achievable - the limitation on a public accommodation for the removal of architectural and communication barriers. It means easily accomplishable and able to be carried out without much difficulty or expense. What is readily achievable for a large, profitable company may not be readily achievable for an economically marginal company.

Undue Burden - means significant difficulty or expense and along with "fundamental alteration" establishes the limitation on a public accommodation with regard to the provision of auxiliary aids and services so as not to discriminate against persons with disabilities.

Public Entity - (A) any State or local government; (B) any department, agency, special purpose district, or other instrumentality of a State or States or local government, and (C) the National Railroad Passenger Corporation, and any commuter authority (as defined in section 103(8) of the Rail Passenger Service Act).

Outline of ADA

Title I	ADA Employment Section
Title II	ADA Public Services and Public Transportation Section
Title III	ADA Public Accommodations and Services Section
Title IV	ADA Telecommunications Section
Title V	ADA Miscellaneous Provisions

Abbreviations

ABA	Architectural Barriers Act of 1968
ADA	Americans with Disability Act of 1990
ADAAG	ADA Accessibility Guidelines for Buildings and Facilities - Appendix "A" to D.O.J. regulation on Title III - (Fed. Reg.7-26-91)
ANSI A117.1	American National Standard for Buildings and Facilities - Providing Accessibility and Useability for Physically Handicapped People - 1986
ATBCB	Architectural and Transportation Barriers Compliance Board
CABO	Council of American Building Officials
CDC	Center for Disease Control
DOT	Department of Transportation
EEOC	Equal Employment Opportunity Commission
FCC	Federal Communications Commission
FHAA	Fair Housing Amendments Act - 1988
MGRAD	Minimum Guidelines and Regulations for Accessible Design (36 CFR part 1190)
Rehab Act	Rehabilitation Act of 1973
UFAS	Uniform Federal Accessibility Standards - 1988

Title I—Employment with Disabilities Fact Sheet

Requirements:

Employers with 15 or more employees may not discriminate against qualified individuals with disabilities. Employers must reasonable accommodate the disabilities of qualified applicants or employees, including modifying work stations and equipment, unless undue hardship would result.

Definitions:

The term "qualified individual with a disability" means an individual with a disability who, with or without reasonable accommodation, can perform the essential functions of the employment position that such individual holds or desires. for the purposes of this title, considerations shall be given to the employers judgment as to what functions of a job are essential, and if an employer has prepared a written description before advertising or interviewing applicants for the job, this description shall be considered evidence of the essential functions of the job.

The term "reasonable accommodation" may include:
(A)making existing facilities used by employees readily accessible to and useable by individuals with disabilities; and
(B)job restructuring, part-time or modified work schedules, reassignment to a vacant position, acquisition or modification of equipment or devices, appropriate adjustment or modifications of examinations, training materials or policies, the provision of qualified readers or interpreters, and other similar accommodations for individuals with disabilities.

In general—The term **"undue hardship"** means:
(A) an action requiring significant difficulty or expense, when considered in light of the factors set forth in subparagraph (B).
(B) Factors to be considered.—In determining whether an accommodation would impose an undue hardship on a covered entity, factors to be considered include:

(i) the nature and cost of the accommodation needed under this Act;

(ii) the overall financial resources of the facility or facilities involved in the provision of the reasonable accommodation; the number of persons employed at such facility; the effect on expenses and resources, or the impact or otherwise of such accommodation upon the operation of the facility;

(iii) the overall financial resources of the covered entity; the overall size of the business of a covered entity with respect to the number of its employees, the number, type, and location of its facilities; and;

(iv) the type of operation or operations of the covered entity including the composition, structure, and functions of the work force of such entity; the geographic separateness, administrative, or fiscal relationship of the facility or facilities in question to the covered entity.

Effective Dates:

July 26, 1992 - for employers with 25 or more employees.
July 26, 1994 - for employers with 15 to 24 employees.

Regulations:

EEOC to issue regulations by July 26, 1991.

Enforcement:

Individuals may file complaints with EEOC. Individuals may also file a private lawsuit after exhausting administrative remedies.

Remedies are the same as available until Title VII of the Civil Rights Act of 1964. Court may order employer to hire or promote qualified individuals, reasonably accommodate their disabilities, and pay back wages and attorneys fees.

Notes:

1. Information presented above was taken from the ATBCB Fact Sheet on ADA dated Nov. 1990.

2. This is not legal advice. A competent lawyer should be consulted regarding any specific legal questions.

June 1991

Title II—Public Entity Facilities Compliance Fact Sheet

General Rule:

No qualified individual with a disability shall be discriminated against or excluded from participation in or the benefits of the services, programs, or activities of a public entity.

Program Accessibility:

No qualified individual with a disability shall, because of inaccessible or unusable facilities of a public entity, be excluded from participation in, or be denied the benefits of the services, programs, or activities of a public entity or be subject to discrimination by any public entity.

Limitations:

It is not required that a public entity take any action that it can demonstrate would constitute a fundamental alteration in the nature of the service, program or activity, or would cause an undue administrative or financial burden. Regardless of that, a public entity is required to take some action that would not trigger this limitation and ensure program accessibility.

Existing Facilities:

A public entity is required to make structural changes to existing facilities only when program accessibility is not feasible any other way (i.e., reassignment of services to accessible building, or provision of auxiliary aids).

Although unable to protect a public entity from complaint or civil suit if programs are not readily accessible to and usable by persons with disabilities by Jan. 26, 1992, each public entity in the U.S. is required to complete a "self-evaluation" of its current policies and practices to identify any non-compliant policies or practices. (See the timetable for Title II facilities compliance on the other side of this sheet).

Where "structural changes" to existing facilities are the only way to arrive at program accessibility, a "transition plan" (only for public entities with 50 employees or more) outlining the steps necessary to complete the structural changes is required. Comments must be invited from disabled persons or organizations representing such individuals. The "transition plan" must be completed by July 26, 1992 and must include the identification of barriers (architectural and communication) to program accessibility, detailed methods for making the facilties accessible, a schedule for implementation and the official responsible for implementation.

New Construction:

All new facilities constructed by, on behalf of or for the use of a public entity shall be designed and constructed to be readily accessible to and usable by persons with disabilities if construction is started or if the invitation for bids is after January 26, 1992.

Alterations:

Alterations to facilities of a public entity must also meet the "readily accessible" standard, to the maximum extent feasible.

Effective Date:

The effective date of this Title is January 26, 1992.

Regulations and Standards:

The Department of Justice issued regulations on July 26, 1991 for all portions of Title II except those portions dealing with Public Transportation which have been issued by the Department of Transportation.

The regulations associated with Title II of the Act and printed in the Federal Register on July 26, 1991 state that compliance with the Uniform Federal Accessibility Standards (UFAS) or the ADAAG (without the elevator exemption) shall satisfy the accessibility requirements of this Title for new and altered buildings and facilities. This publication also states that "departures from particular requirements of those standards by use of other methods shall be permitted when it is clearly evident that equivalent access to the facility or part of the facility is thereby provided."

Most facilities constructed or altered with Federal funds are presently required to comply with UFAS under the Architectural Barriers Act of 1968. Facilities constructed or altered by recipients of Federal financial assistance are presently required to comply with UFAS under Section 504 of the Rehabiliation Act of 1973.

Enforcement:

Those who believe themselves discriminated against may file a civil lawsuit in Federal District Court.

Individuals may file complaints with the designated Federal agencies concerning matters of Title II discrimination or contact the Department of Justice who will direct the complaints as required. The Federal agency specified in the regulations will then investigate the complaint (if made within 180 days of the alleged discrimination), attempt to resolve complaints on a voluntary compliance basis and then, if unsuccessful, refer case to the Department of Justice for civil suit.

Remedies are the same as available under Section 505 of the Rehabilitation Act of 1973. Courts may order an entity to make facilities accessible, provide auxiliary aids or services, modify policies, and pay attorneys' fees.

Notes:

Unless stated otherwise, information presented above was taken from the Title II regulations published by the D.O.J. in the Federal Register July 26, 1991.

This is not legal advice. A competent lawyer should be consulted regarding any specific legal questions.

Evan Terry Associates, P.C. / 2129 Montgomery Highway / Birmingham, Alabama 35209 / (205) 871-9765 / ©1992

Title II—Public Entity Facilities Compliance Timetable

7-26-1990

Signing of the Americans with Disabilities Act of 1990 by President George Bush.

2-28-1991

Draft Regulations issued by the Department of Justice for implementing Title II.

4-29-1991

Final comments on draft regulations due at DOJ.

7-26-1991

Final regulations for implementing Title II published by the Department of Justice.

1-26-1992
Effective Date of Title II

1.) Ensure that the operation of each service, program and activity is operating so that each, when viewed in its entirety, is readily accessible to and usable by individuals with disabilities. (35.150(a))

Even though the following required procedures will not shield a public entity from a discrimination complaint, they are mandatory if programs are not readily accessible to and usable by people with disabilities:

  A. Begin self-evaluation process for those areas of services, policies and practices not previously evaluated (and on file) for section 504 of the Rehabilitation Act of 1973. (35.105)

  B. Begin transition plan outlining structural changes required for program accessibility and proceed with structural changes, as required, to facilities "as expeditiously as possible". (35.150(c))

2.) New construction starting after this date must be readily accessible. (35.151(a))

3.) The altered portions of alterations beginning construction after this date must, to the maximum extent feasible, meet the readily accessible to and usable by individuals with disabilities standard set by the Uniform Federal Accessibility Standard or, at the public entity's option, the ADAAG. (35.151(b))

4.) Date a complaint or civil law suit may be filed by an individual based on ADA discrimination by a public entity.

7-26-1992

Transition plan complete where structural changes to facilities will be undertaken to provide program access. Transition plan must identify obstacles, describe in detail the methods that will be used to make facilities accessible, specify the schedule for taking the steps identified and indicate the official responsible for implementation of the plan. (35.150(d))

1-26-1993

Self-evaluation complete. (35.105(a))

1-26-1995

Completion of last structural changes to facilities where such changes were undertaken for program accessibility.(35.150(c))

This is not legal advice. A competent lawyer should be consulted regarding any specific legal questions. Information presented above was taken from D.O.J.Regulation (28CFR Part 35) on Title II of ADA.

Evan Terry Associates, P.C. / 2129 Montgomery Highway / Birmingham, Alabama 35209 / (205) 871-9765 / ©1992

 ADA Facilities Compliance™
7-92

Title III—Public Accommodation (Facilities) Fact Sheet

Purpose of the Act:
Address the concerns of the 43 million Americans that have one or more physical or mental disabilities and are faced each day with architectural/transportation barriers, overprotective rules and policies, intentional exclusion and relegation to lesser services, programs, activities, benefits, jobs and other opportunities.

General Rule:
No individuals shall be discriminated against on the basis of disabilities in the full and equal enjoyment of goods, services, facilities, privileges, advantages or accommodations at any place of public accommodation by any person who owns, leases or operates a place of public accommodation.

Benefits provided for the disabled cannot be separate or different from those provided for others, unless they are as effective as those provided for others.

It is discriminatory to exclude an individual who has a relationship or association with one who is disabled from the equal enjoyment of goods, services, facilities, privileges, advantages or accommodations or other opportunities afforded other individuals.

Existing Facilities:
Architectural and communication barriers that are structural in nature in existing facilities must be removed on or before Jan. 26, 1992 where such removal is readily achievable. If these are not readily achievable then alternative methods must be provided, if they are readily achievable.

Auxiliary aids and services must be offered those with disabilities to ensure that they are not excluded, denied services, segregated or otherwise treated differently from others, unless it can be shown that taking such steps would alter the fundamental nature of the benefit or would result in an undue burden.

New Construction:
All new construction must be readily accessible to and usable by individuals with disabilities if the first occupancy is after January 26, 1993 and the last application for a building permit is certified as complete after Jan. 26, 1992 unless it can be demonstrated that it is structurally impracticable.

Alterations:
All altered portions of an existing facility must, to the maximum extent feasible, be made readily accessible to and usable by individuals with disabilities. If a primary function area is altered, the path of travel including restrooms, public telephones and drinking fountains serving that area must also be made readily accessible except where alterations to the path of travel are disproportionate (more than 20% of cost of the overall alterations project). Elevators are required in all new facilities except those less than 3 stories or those with less than 3000 s.f. per floor (shopping centers and professional offices of health care providers are not exempt, nor are airport passenger terminals or other stations used for specified public transportation.

Regulations and Standards:
The Attorney General issued regulations associated with this portion on July 26, 1991. ATBCB issued the ADA Accessibility Guidelines on that same day.

Exemptions:
The Act does not apply to private clubs or establishments exempted from coverage under Title II of the Civil Rights Act of 1964, nor does it apply to religious organizations or entities controlled by religious organizations. Residential buildings, covered or not by FHAA, and Federal Buildings, covered by ABA, are also exempt from ADA.

Enforcement:
Those who believe themselves discriminated against may file a civil suit for injunctive relief limited to an order to alter the facilities to make them readily accessible to and usable by the disabled and/or the requirement of auxiliary aids or services, modification of a policies or the provision of alternative methods, to the extent required by law. The U.S. Attorney General has the power to investigate alleged violations and file suit for appropriate relief including monetary (but not punitive) damages and civil penalties up to $50,000 for the first violation and $100,000 for any subsequent violation.

Where appropriate and to the extent authorized by law, the use of alternative means of dispute resolution including settlement negotiations, conciliation, facilitation, mediation, fact finding, minitrials and arbitration is encouraged to resolve disputes arising under this Act.

Effective Dates:
In general, the effective date of this Title of the ADA Law will be January 26, 1992. Smaller businesses are given either six months or a year extension depending on their size and their previous year's gross receipts.

All new construction with first occupancy after January 26, 1993 shall comply with the provisions of this Act. All alterations to existing facilities shall, to the maximum extent feasible, be made readily accessible to and usable by the disabled if construction begins after January 26, 1992.

Notes:
1. Information presented above was taken from D.O.J. Title III Regulations and U.S. Public Law 101-336, July 26, 1990.
2. Limited tax credits are available to small businesses who make accommodations accessible to the disabled. Tax deductions for the removal of barriers to the disabled, allowed under IRC-190, were reduced in October 1990 to $15,000. An accountant should be consulted.
3. This is not legal advice. A competent lawyer should be consulted regarding any specific legal questions.

This document may be reproduced without permission if credit is given to Evan Terry Associates, P.C.

Evan Terry Associates, P.C. / 2129 Montgomery Highway / Birmingham, Alabama 35209 / (205) 871-9765 / ©1991

ADA Facilities Compliance™
7-92

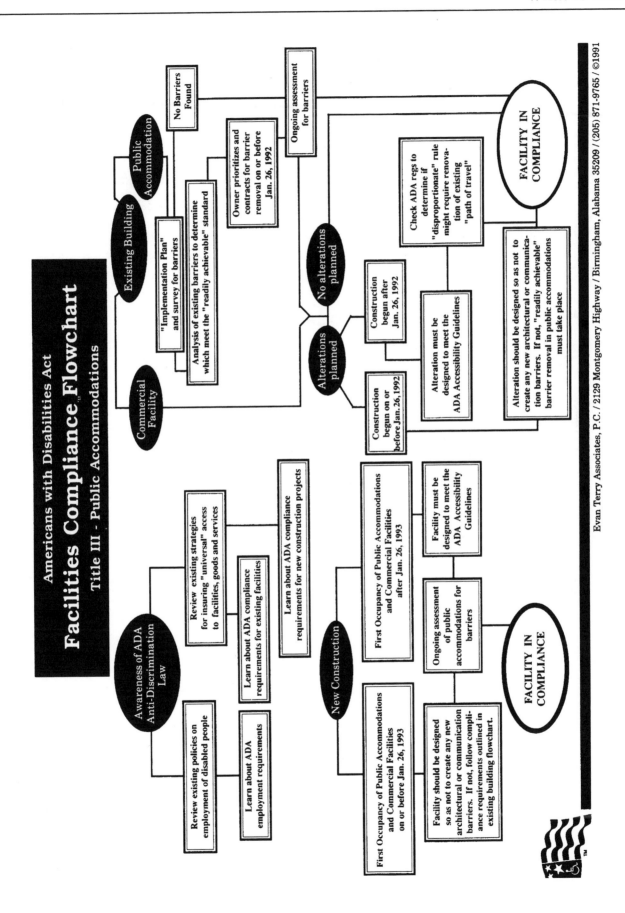

Americans with Disabilities Act
Facilities Compliance Flowchart™
Title III - Public Accommodations

Awareness of ADA Anti-Discrimination Law

Review existing policies on employment of disabled people

Learn about ADA employment requirements

Review existing strategies for insuring "universal" access to facilities, goods and services

Learn about ADA compliance requirements for existing facilities

Learn about ADA compliance requirements for new construction projects

Existing Building

Public Accommodation

No Barriers Found

"Implementation Plan" and survey for barriers

Analysis of existing barriers to determine which meet the "readily achievable" standard

Owner prioritizes and contracts for barrier removal on or before Jan. 26, 1992

Ongoing assessment for barriers

Commercial Facility

Alterations planned

No alterations planned

Construction begun on or before Jan. 26, 1992

Construction begun after Jan. 26, 1992

Alteration must be designed to meet the ADA Accessibility Guidelines

Check ADA regs to determine if "disproportionate" rule might require renovation of existing "path of travel"

Alteration should be designed so as not to create any new architectural or communication barriers. If not, "readily achievable" barrier removal in public accommodations must take place

FACILITY IN COMPLIANCE

New Construction

First Occupancy of Public Accommodations and Commercial Facilities on or before Jan. 26, 1993

First Occupancy of Public Accommodations and Commercial Facilities after Jan. 26, 1993

Facility should be designed so as not to create any new architectural or communication barriers. If not, follow compliance requirements outlined in existing building flowchart.

Facility must be designed to meet the ADA Accessibility Guidelines

Ongoing assessment of public accommodations for barriers

FACILITY IN COMPLIANCE

Evan Terry Associates, P.C. / 2129 Montgomery Highway / Birmingham, Alabama 35209 / (205) 871-9765 / ©1991

ADA Facilities Compliance™
7-92

Title IV—Telecommunications Provisions Fact Sheet

Requirements:

Telephone companies must provide telecommunications relay services for hearing-impaired and speech-impaired individuals 24 hours per day.

Effective Date:

By July 26, 1994.

Regulations:

FCC to issue regulations by July 26, 1991.

Enforcement:

Individuals may file complaints with the FCC.

Notes:

1. Information presented above was taken from the ATBCB Fact Sheet on ADA dated Nov. 1990.
2. This is not legal advice. A competent lawyer should be consulted regarding any specific legal questions.

June 1991

Evan Terry Associates, P.C. / 2129 Montgomery Highway / Birmingham, Alabama 35209 / (205) 871-9765 / ©1992

Title V—Miscellaneous Provisions Fact Sheet

General:

If there are more stringent Federal, state, or local laws with regard to issues of this act they shall supersede this act.

Immunity:

States shall not be immune under the eleventh amendment for a violation of this Act.

Retaliation:

No person shall discriminate against any individual because they opposed any act or practice made unlawful by this Act.

Issuance of Guidelines:

Not later than 9 months after date of enactment of Act: the Architectural and Transportation Barriers Compliance board shall issue minimum guidelines. (ADAAG)

Contents of Guidelines:

ADAAG shall establish requirements to ensure that buildings, and transportation are consistent with this Act.

Qualified Historic Properties:

The guidelines shall include procedures and requirements for alterations to Historic Buildings.

Attorneys Fees:

The court may allow the prevailing party, other than United States a reasonable attorneys fee, including expenses.

Technical Assistance:

Plan - not later than 180 days after enactment of Act the Attorney General shall develop a plan to assist entities and agencies covered under this Act.

Congress:

Congress and the Agencies of the Legislative Branch are committed to the implementation and compliance of this Act and are not exempt.

Technical Assistance Manuals:

Each Federal agency that has responsibility under this Act shall ensure the availability of appropriate technical manuals to individuals or entities with rights under this Act no later than six months after final regulations are published. Each Federal agency that has responsibly under this Act may make grants or award contracts to individuals, institutions subject to the availability of funds.

Federal Wilderness Areas:

National Council on Disability shall conduct a study and report on the ability of individuals with disabilities to use and enjoy the National Wilderness Preservation System.

Transvestites:

For the purposes of this Act, the term "disabled" or "disability" shall not apply to an individual solely because that individual is a transvestite.

Illegal use of Drugs:

For the purpose of this Act, the term "individual with a disability" does not include an individual who is currently engaging in the illegal use of drugs.

Severability:

Should any provision in this Act be found unconstitutional by a court of law, such provision shall be severed from the remainder of the Act.

Amendments to the Rehabilitation Act - 1973:

Among other things ADA modified the Rehab. Act so with regard to employment, the term "individual with a handicap" does, now, not include a person who is an alcoholic if the current use of alcohol prevents that person from doing his/her job or if his/her job is one in which current alcohol abuse would "constitute a direct threat to property or the safety of others."

Notes:

1. Information presented above was taken from the ATBCB Fact Sheet on ADA dated Nov. 1990.
2. This is not legal advice. A competent lawyer should be consulted regarding any specific legal questions.

June 1991

Evan Terry Associates, P.C. / 2129 Montgomery Highway / Birmingham, Alabama 35209 / (205) 871-9765 / ©1992

ADA Facilities Compliance™
7-92

Issues of Title II and Title III

Introduction

As you will soon read, **Title II** states that no qualified disabled individual may be denied the benefits of services, programs, or activities by state or local governments or their agencies, nor be excluded from participation in those benefits, and **Title III prohibits discrimination** against those with disabilities through the denial of an equal opportunity to "participate in or benefit from the goods, services, facilities, privileges, advantages, or accommodations of an entity", as the law states. Although a portion of Title III addresses issues associated with public transportation offered by private entities, we will not deal with this topic as our focus is primarily upon facilities compliance.

Although this act (the ADA) may appear overwhelming, given time it is **fairly easy** to understand, and will probably not result in massive expenditures for corrective or compliance work. The essence of the facility compliance requirements of Title II and Title III is that disabled individuals are and have been discriminated against because the design of our buildings pose "barriers" for them and they do not have the same opportunities to play, learn, work and travel as those who are not disabled. This Law prohibits this discrimination. The facilities issues of Title II hinge around the requirement that all public entities ensure that the programs that are offered are accessible to all people. The facilities issues of Title III can be broken down into three (3) main areas, each of which will need to be reviewed if you wish to limit your exposure to civil suits. These main areas of concern include barriers in existing facilities, issues associated with alterations and issues associated with new construction.

The first of the three main areas of Title III which you need to understand applies only to places of public accommodation and is the **"readily achievable removal of architectural and communication barriers"**. Architectural barriers in this context include, among other things, street curbs without ramps, narrow door ways, the lack of grab bars in restrooms, and small flights of stairs without an accessible ramp. Communication barriers include, among other things, public telephones mounted too high for use by those in wheelchairs, fire alarms that do not have flashing strobe alert features, a lack of braille symbols at elevator control panels, and so forth.

The second area of concern to you under Title III is building or facilities **"alterations"** to either public accommodations or commercial facilities. It is required by ADA, to design and construct alterations and/or renovations to the "maximum extent feasible" so that they are "readily accessible to and usable by the disabled". There are also considerations with regard to alterations that may require the renovation of areas used to access your proposed altered space.

The third and last area of concern regarding facilities under Title III deals with the compliance issues for **"new construction"**. As with alterations and renovations, new construction shall be "readily accessible to and usable by" those with disabilities. This may be the least difficult issue of the three, because in many states architects have been required for years to design buildings to meet certain minimum accessibility requirements.

You should be aware that among these three different facility compliance requirement types, there are two standards of care to which compliance will be judged. The **"greater standard"** is that required in alterations and new construction projects which demand that the space be "readily accessible to and usable by" the disabled. The **"lesser standard"** is that required in the removal of architectural and communication barriers which must be "readily achievable".

Before we go into detail on the facility compliance requirements of Titles II and III, I think we must have a better understanding of what the law means when it says "person with a disability".

Disability Defined

As you may have found, the main thrust of the **American's with Disabilities Act** is to protect those who are disabled from discrimination based upon their disability. Although, we are only touching upon Title I and Title II, (which deal with employment issues and state and local government issues respectively), they protect those who are "qualified individuals with a disability". The law defines that phrase as follows:

> **QUALIFIED INDIVIDUAL WITH A DISABILITY.**
> The term "qualified individual with a disability" means an individual with a disability who, with or without reasonable modifications to rules, policies, or

practices, the removal of architectural, communication, or transportation barriers, or the provision of auxiliary aids and services, meets the essential eligibility requirements for the receipt of services or the participation in programs or activities provided by a public entity.

Under ADA Title III, those with disabilities are protected "on the basis of disability". This leads us to the question, what is the definition of a disability? ADA defines **disability** as it relates to an individual as follows:

(a) A physical or mental impairment that **substantially limits** one or more of the major life activities of such individual;

(b) A record of such impairment; or

(c) Being regarded as having an impairment.

Note that the law categorizes disabilities into two "umbrella" terms. Those being **"physical impairments"** and **"mental impairments"** which have their original definition under the regulations issued for Section 504 of the Rehabilitation Act of 1973.

Section 504 also defines **"major life activities"** as "functions such as caring for one's self, performing manual tasks, walking, seeing, hearing, speaking, breathing, learning, and working ....", which was also echoed in the Senate and House Committee reports on ADA.

Under the "umbrella" term of **"physical impairment"**, the National Council on Disability offers two other sub-categories: sensory (such as vision or hearing impairments), and physical (such as orthopedic and neuromotor disabilities). Under the **"mental impairments"**, the National Council of Disability offers the following sub-categories: cognitive (including mental retardation and learning disabilities) and mental or emotional disabilities.

Although, under Title I of this Act, the disabled individual must show that their particular condition is a physical or mental impairment which substantially limits one or more major life activities, the Title III portion of the law does not make this requirement, but assumes that there are those individuals with such disabilities and requires that facilities be designed, constructed and modified to accommodate them.

The Bureau of National Affairs in their publication, "The Americans with Disabilities Act" states the following:

Action by regulatory agencies or legislatures, or proof presented by litigants in circumstances of particular cases has resulted in the following conditions being declared physical or mental impairments that substantially limit a major life activity.

VISION IMPAIRMENTS—Blindness, legal blindness, retinitis pigmentosa, and vision in only one eye.

HEARING IMPAIRED—Deafness, impaired hearing and use of hearing aids, and "bilateral, sensory-neural hearing loss".

EMOTIONAL DISTURBANCE AND MENTAL ILLNESS—"Psychiatric problems" and inability to handle stressful situations, schizophrenia, depressive neurosis, manic depressive syndrome, paranoid schizophrenia, childhood schizophrenia, "emotional illness", "chronic mental illness", "severe psychiatric difficulties", and "serious emotional disturbance".

SEIZURE DISORDERS—Epilepsy.

MENTAL RETARDATION—"Mental retardation", "educable mental retardation" and "profound or severe mental retardation".

ORTHOPEDIC OR NEUROMOTOR DISABILITIES— Use of a wheelchair, paraplegia, "mobility handicapped" or "mobility disabled", "cognitive limb deficiency", multiple sclerosis, cerebral palsy, muscular dystrophy, chondroblastic dwarfism, spina bifida, back injury resulting in inability to lift heavy weights, degenerative spinal condition, "severe lumbosacral sacroiliac sprain with radioculopathy" (sic), limited mobility of arm and shoulder, osteoarthritis in the hip, amputated leg, and artificial leg.

SPEECH IMPAIRMENTS—Speech impairments.

LEARNING DISABILITIES—Learning disability or "specific learning disability", dyslexia, and "calligraphic dysgraphia and dyslexia".

OTHER SERIOUS HEALTH IMPAIRMENTS—Diabetes, heart disease, "arteriosclerotic heart disease and angina pectoris", "nervous condition and heart condition", cancer, mastectomy, lung disease, asthma, cystic fibrosis, absence or removal of a kidney, hepatitis B carrier, narcolepsy, HIV infection, asbestosis and asbestos-related diseases, intolerance to contact cement and other hydro carbon fumes, Crohn's disease, alcoholism, and drug addiction or abuse.

Although the list above may be useful in trying to understand the broad spectrum of disabilities that have been used in Federal Disability Non-Discrimination Legislation, it is probable that conditions that are **not** listed above will be brought to light in future Federal non-discrimination legislation and the absence of a particular condition from the above list does not suggest that it is not a disability covered under ADA.

It is important to note that a number of conditions are excluded from the ADA definition of "disabled". In Section 511(b) of ADA the following conditions are defined and are not included in the definition of the term "disability":

1. Transvestism, transsexualism, pedophilia, exhibitionism, voyeurism, gender identity disorders not resulting from physical impairments, or other sexual behavior disorders;

2. Compulsive gambling, kleptomania, or pyromania; or

3. Psychoactive substance use disorders resulting from current illegal use of drugs.

Section 511 (a) states that homosexuality and bisexuality are "not impairments" and thus are not to be considered disabilities under the Act.

Now that we know what the law means by the term "disability", we can study specifically what the facility requirements are for Title II and Title III. If you will recall from our chapter "What Is ADA?" you should focus on Title II if you represent a "public entity" and on Title III if you represent a "private entity". There are great differences in the compliance requirements for Title II and Title III facilities, therefore, if you are unclear, go back and study the differences.

Mandate for Public Entities Title II

The primary anti-discrimination mandate with regard to facilities operated by a public entity is found in Section 202 and reads as follows:

DISCRIMINATION—Subject to the provisions of this Title, no qualified individual with a disability shall, by reason of such disability be excluded from participation in or be denied the benefits of the services, programs, or activities of a public entity, or be subjected to discrimination by such entity.

This means that we need to address the definition of "Public Entity". The Law defines it as follows:

PUBLIC ENTITY—The term "public entity" means

(A) any State or local government

(B) any department, agency, special purpose district, or other instrumentality of a State or States or local government, and

(C) the National Railroad Passenger Corporation, and any commuter authority (as defined in section 103(8) of the Rail Passenger Service Act).

Although Title II includes issues relative to employment, transportation and other non-facilities oriented concerns, we will focus our discussion only on those issues related to accessible facilities as provided by state and local government services. The primary concern of Title II is related to "program accessibility". Program accessibility as outlined in the regulations dated July 26, 1991 and published by the Justice Department includes two primary concerns: 1.) existing facilities and 2.) new construction and alterations.

Self-Evaluation—Title II

The requirements for a public entity to make a self-evaluation stems from Section 504 of the Rehabilitation Act of 1973 and is set forth under Section 35.105 of the Title II ADA regulations. The regulations state the following about that section:

All public entities are required to do a self-evaluation. However, only those that employ 50 or more persons are required to maintain the self-evaluation on file and make it available for public inspection for **three years**.

Paragraph (d) provides that the self-evaluation required by this section shall apply only to programs not subject to section 504 or those policies and practices, such as those involving communications access, that have not already been included in a self-evaluation required under an existing regulation implementing section 504. Because most self-evaluations were done from five to twelve years ago, however, the **Department expects that a great many public entities will be reexamining all of their policies and programs. Programs and functions may have changed, and actions that were supposed to have been taken to comply with section 504 may not have been fully implemented or may no longer be effective**. In addition, there have been statutory amendments to section 504 which have changed the coverage of section 504, particularly the Civil Rights Restoration Act of 1987, Public Law No. 100-259, 102 Stat. 28 (1988), which broadened the definition of a covered "program or activity."

As you have had a chance to review the effective dates for Title II in the previous chapter, you may be wondering if the requirement for self-evaluation, which doesn't have to be complete until twelve-months after the January 26, 1992 effective date, will shield a public entity from complaints or civil suits. The answer is no. It will not shield a public entity from complaint or civil suit, but it is required nonetheless. To elaborate further, the preamble to the regulation addresses this concern:

> Several commenters (to the proposed regulations) suggested that the Department clarify public entities' liability during the one-year period for compliance with the self-evaluation requirement. The self-evaluation requirement does not stay the effective date of the statute nor of this part. Public entities are, therefore, not shielded from discrimination claims during that time.

> Other commenters suggested that the rule require that every self-evaluation include an examination of training efforts to assure that individuals with disabilities are not subjected to discrimination because of insensitivity, particularly in the law enforcement area. Although the Department has not added such a specific requirement to the rule, it would be appropriate for public entities to evaluate training efforts because, in many cases, lack of training leads to discriminatory practices, even when the policies in place are nondiscriminatory.

Existing Title II Facilities

With regard to existing state and local governmental facilities, Title II does not necessarily require the removal of architectural barriers as is required of public accommodations under Title III because of the "inherent flexibility of the program accessibility requirement" of Title II, as stated in the preamble to the Regulations on this title. Title II requires only that the public entity ensure that all of its programs are accessible when viewed in their entirety. The regulations state it more clearly:

> The regulation makes clear, however, that a public entity is not required to make each of its existing facilities accessible (section 35.150(a)(1)). Unlike title III of the Act, which requires public accommodations to remove architectural barriers where such removal is "readily achievable," or to provide goods and services through alternative methods, where those methods are "readily achievable," **title II requires a public entity to make its programs accessible in all cases, except where to do so would result in a fundamental alteration in the nature of the program or in undue financial and administrative burdens**. Congress intended the "undue burden" standard in title II to be significantly higher than the "readily achievable" standard in title III. Thus, although title II may not require removal of barriers in some cases where removal would be required under title III, the program access requirement of title II should enable individuals with disabilities to participate in and benefit from the services, programs, or activities of public entities **in all but the most unusual cases**.

Methods of providing this **program accessibility** include among others the following: redesigning equipment, reassignment of services to accessible buildings, assignment of aids to beneficiaries, home visits, delivery of services to alternative accessible sites, alteration of existing facilities and construction of new facilities, use of accessible rolling stock or other conveyances, or, as stated in the regulations "any other methods that result in making its services, programs, or activities readily accessible to and usable by individuals with disabilities". A public entity is not required under Title II to ensure program accessibility solely through **structural changes** in existing facilities if other methods are effective in providing program accessibility. The preamble included in the regulations states the following:

Structural changes in existing facilities are required only when there is no other feasible way to make a public entity's program accessible. (It should be noted that "structural changes" include all physical changes to a facility; the term does not refer only to changes to structural features, such as removal of or alteration to a load bearing structural member.)

Where structural changes to existing facilities are elected by a public entity as the method of providing program access for all people, a **"transition plan"** outlining how the changes will be done is required. This requirement is for public entities with 50 or more employees only.

The transition plan is the same as that required for compliance with Section 504 of the Rehabilitation Act and if a transition plan is already in effect based on a previous compliance requirement such as this, then only programs not already covered by those plans will be required to comply.

What makes up a transition plan? Each transition plan must include at least the following components:

(i) Identify physical obstacles in the public entity's facilities that limit the accessibility of its programs or activities to individuals with disabilities;

(ii) Describe in detail the methods that will be used to make the facilities accessible;

(iii) Specify the schedule for taking the steps necessary to achieve compliance with this section and, if the time period of the transition plan is longer than one year, identify steps that will be taken during each year of the transition period; and

(iv) Indicate the official responsible for implementation of the plan.

Interested parties, including people with disabilities, shall have an opportunity to participate in the formulation of the transition plan by being given a chance to comment. The plan must be made available for public inspection. This transition plan must be completed within six months of the January 26, 1992 effective date. Structural changes must be made as "expeditiously as possible" but by no later than 1-26-95.

With regard to existing Title II facilities, the regulations do not require any public entity to "take any action that it can demonstrate would result in a fundamental alteration in the nature of a service, program, or activity or in undue financial and administrative burdens". It is required that the public entity prove that this action would either result in a fundamental alteration or be an undue financial or administrative burden and it is the responsibility of the head of the public entity to provide a written statement of all the reasons that were compiled in reaching that conclusion. It is very important to note that even though a particular action might result in an alteration of the fundamental nature of a service, program, or activity or in the undue financial or administrative burden of that public entity, the public entity is required "nevertheless (to) ensure that individuals with disabilities receive the benefits or services provided by the public entity".

It is interesting to note that the Department of Justice states the following with regard to that anticipated defense by a public entity, "compliance ..... would in most cases not result in **undue financial and administrative burdens** on a public entity. In determining whether financial and administrative burdens are undue, all public entity resources available for use in the funding and operation of the service, program, or activity should be considered."

New and Altered Title II Facilities

Title II requires that all new buildings, facilities or parts of facilities constructed "by, on behalf of, or for the use of a public entity shall be designed and constructed in such manner that the facility or part of the facility is readily accessible to and usable by individuals with disabilities ....."

Regarding alterations to state and local governmental facilities that affect or could affect the usability of that facility, the alteration shall be, to the maximum extent feasible, undertaken so as to ensure that the altered portion of the facility is "readily accessible to and usable by" individuals with disabilities.

In existing buildings that are leased by a public entity after January 26, 1992, the regulations state that they are "not required by the regulation to meet the accessibility standard simply by virtue of being leased. They are subject, however, to the program accessibility standard for existing facilities in Section 35.150. To the extent the buildings are newly constructed or altered they must also meet the new construction and alteration requirements of Section 35.151." The regulations go on to state that the federal practice under Section 504 of the Rehabilitation Act of 1973 has always treated newly leased buildings as if they were existing facilities and held to the program accessibility standard. The regulations state the following:

Unlike the construction of new buildings where architectural barriers can be avoided at little or no cost, the application of new construction standards to an existing building being leased raises the same prospect of retrofitting buildings as the use of an existing federal facility, and the same program accessibility should apply to both owned and leased existing buildings.

Pursuant to the requirements for leased buildings contained in the Minimum Guidelines for Accessible Design published under the Architectural Barriers Act by the Architectural and Transportation Barriers Compliance Board, 36CFR 1190.34, the federal government may not lease a building unless it contains (1) an accessible route from an accessible entrance to those areas in which the principal activities for which the building is leased are conducted, (2) accessible toilet facilities and (3) accessible parking facilities if a parking area is included within the lease. Although these requirements are not applicable to buildings leased by public entities covered by this regulation, such entities are encouraged to look for the most accessible space available to lease and to attempt to find space complying at least with these minimum federal requirements.

Communications—Title II

Further considerations under Title II that may affect a public entities' facilities include the requirement that appropriate steps be taken to ensure that communications with applicants, members of the public and participants that may be disabled are as effective as communications offered to others, secondly that auxiliary aids appropriate to the individual be made available to afford an individual with disabilities "an equal opportunity to participate in, and enjoy the benefits of, a service, program or activity conducted by a public entity". Also, telecommunication devices for the deaf, TDD(s) are required where state and local governmental agencies communicate with beneficiaries or applicants by telephone to ensure equal service to participants that may be hearing impaired or speech impaired. Alternative telecommunication systems might also be utilized if they afforded an equally effective communication opportunity to persons with disabilities. It is also interesting to note that under Title II, "911" emergency telephone services must provide to individuals that use TDD's or computer modems the same service that is provided to other telephone users.

Signage—Title II

Building signs are an important part of all facilities and every public entity is required to provide signage concerning accessible programs, activities, facilities and at all inaccessible entrances directing users to accessible entrances or locations where they can obtain information about alternative accessible facilities. In addition, each accessible entrance to a facility must have a sign bearing the international symbol for accessibility.

Accessibility Standards—Title II

New construction and alteration projects by, on the behalf of or for the use of a public entity whose construction is commenced after January 26, 1992 must comply with the requirements of Title II and shall be held to the accessibility standard of the Uniform Federal Accessibility Standards or the ADA Accessibility Guidelines. Currently, almost all facilities constructed or altered with federal funds are required to comply with UFAS under the Architectural Barriers Act of 1968. Facilities constructed or altered by recipients of federal financial assistance are also presently required to comply with UFAS under Section 504 of the Rehabilitation Act of 1973.

Transportation—Title II

For more information on facility design requirements for bus stops, train and mass transit stations, airport terminals, and boat and ferry docks, please refer to the supplemental guidelines published in the Federal Register on Friday, September 6, 1991 by the Architectural and Transportation Barriers Compliance Board and the D.O.T. regulations published the same day.

Summary—Title II

In summary, if you remember nothing else about the facility accessibility issues of Title II, remember this:

1. All State and Local Government programs are covered.

2. Program Accessibility requires changes to existing buildings only if no other administrative option is chosen.

3. Until the final supplement to MGRAD is issued, UFAS or, at the entity's option, ADAAG is the accessibility standard.

4. Every State or Local Government agency will have to make a "self-evaluation" of their program accessibility (see Chapter on Compliance Strategies") which may include a detailed transition plan.

Historic Buildings—Title II

With regard to existing historic preservation programs, the regulations state that a public entity shall give priority to programs that allow physical access to individuals with disabilities but in cases where alterations would result in a substantial loss or impairment of "significant historic features of an historic property" or would "result in a fundamental alteration in the nature of a service, program or activity, or in undue financial and administrative burdens", then the following alternative methods of choosing program accessibility would be acceptable.

1. Using audiovisual materials and devices to depict those portions of an historic property that cannot otherwise be made accessible;

2. assigning persons to guide individuals with disabilities into or through portions of historic properties that cannot otherwise be made accessible; or

3. adopting other innovative methods.

Mandate for Public Accommodations Title III

Before we go into the "meat" of Title III, which as you will recall deals with "private entities", we must consider a couple of critical terms. We begin with the terms that define the occupancy of the facility or portion of the facility—Public Accommodations and Commercial Facilities.

Public Accommodations

The term **"public accommodations"** is the central focus of Title III. A deeper understanding of this term will lead to a better appreciation for the intent behind the law. The law defines **"public accommodations"** as follows:

> **Public Accommodations**—The following **private entities** are considered public accommodations for the purposes of this Title, if the operations of such entities affect commerce—
>
> (a) an inn, hotel, motel, or other place of lodging except for an establishment located within a building that contains not more than five rooms for rent or hire and that is actually occupied by the proprietor of such establishment as the residence of such proprietor;
>
> (b) a restaurant, bar or other establishment serving food or drink;

(c) a motion picture house, theater, concert hall, stadium or other place of exhibition or entertainment;

(d) an auditorium, convention center, lecture hall or other place of public gathering;

(e) a bakery, grocery store, clothing store, hardware store, shopping center or other sales or rental establishment;

(f) a laundromat, dry cleaner, bank, barber shop, beauty shop, travel service, shoe repair service, funeral parlor, gas station, office of an accountant or lawyer, pharmacy, insurance office, professional office of a healthcare provider, hospital, or other service establishment;

(g) a terminal depot or other station used for specified public transportation;

(h) a museum, library, gallery, or other place of public display or collection;

(i) a park, zoo, amusement park or other place of recreation;

(j) a nursery, elementary, secondary, undergraduate, or post graduate private school or other place of education;

(k) a day care center, senior citizen's center, homeless shelter, food bank, adoption agency or other social service center establishment;

(l) a gymnasium, health spa, bowling alley, golf course or other place of exercise or recreation.

The list above is just a partial list of the possible places that are covered under the term **"public accommodations"** and certainly does not cover all possible options. For a broader definition, we can refer to the House Judicial Committee Report which defines the 12 categories of **public accommodations** as follows:

The bill ..... provides examples of public accommodations, based on the following categories: (1) places of lodging; (2) establishments serving food or drink; (3) places of exhibition or entertainment; (4) places of public gathering; (5) establishments selling or renting items; (6) establishments providing services; (7) stations used for public transportation; (8) places of public display or collection; (9) places of recreation; (10) places of education; (11) establishments providing social services; and (12) places of exercise or recreation.

In a rather confusing twist, the ADA regulations suggest, so as to be consistent with section 302(a) of the law, the statutory definition as well as the congressional report definition actually identify a **"place of public accommodation"** and the actual **"public accommodation"** is applied to the "private entity that owns, leases (or leases to), or operates a place of public accommodation."

Entities not falling under one of these categories or not privately operated or not affecting commerce are not considered to be public accommodations. Entities that are not public accommodations, may be commercial facilities and subject to the new construction and alteration requirements of Section 303 of the law. Entities operated by governments are not covered by this title, but are covered by other titles of this bill and other federal laws. The fact that a private entity receives funds from federal, state, or local governments, would not remove it from coverage under this title.

Neither the place of public accommodation nor the programs and services offered by the public accommodation can discriminate against individuals with disabilities. As discussed below, there is an obligation not to discriminate in programs and services provided by the public accommodation, to remove barriers in existing facilities, and to make new and altered facilities accessible and usable. It is not sufficient to only make facilities accessible and usable; this title prohibits as well, discrimination in the provision of programs and activities conducted by the public accommodation.

As you can see from the above categories, the term **"public accommodations"** applies to most of the non-residential facilities in this country open to the general public. Compliance with the regulations of Title III of the ADA will allow people with disabilities access to a tremendous number of facilities that heretofore may have been inaccessible. You may also begin to understand the depth and far-reaching consequences of this law as you ponder the number of existing and contemplated public facilities around the country.

Commercial Facilities

Commercial facilities are defined as those facilities "that are intended for non-residential use by a **private entity** and whose operations will affect commerce". You should also use the 12 categories listed previously for the identification of public accommodations as a test to see if your facility is designated properly.

Commercial facilities are not covered under the general rules of Section 302 which relate to discrimination (ie. the removal of barriers) in public accommodation, but are covered under Section 303 which deals with the accessibility of new construction and altered portions of existing facilities. Like public accommodations, these facilities may also be covered under the requirements of Title I—Employment Issues, and a review of the requirements of disabled employees and job applicants as they relate to your commercial facilities is required under Title I. See also the notes on **"reasonable accommodations"** addressed further in this chapter and be aware that new and altered commercial facilities are going to be judged by the "greater standard" of "readily accessible to and usable by" the disabled.

Examples of **commercial facilities** might include manufacturing facilities, processing facilities, industrial facilities, certain office buildings, and other buildings where employment occurs.

The regulations frequently mention the situation where a building might be considered a mix-use facility. Not only mixed in terms of having public accommodation portions and commercial facility portions, but also commercial facilities in residences or in exempt church buildings or in apartments covered by FHAA. In each of these cases the specific requirements of each occupancy type would hold true for that portion of the facilities (i.e., barrier removal in only public accommodations not the exempt portions).

An illustration of the mixed-use facility might be a facility not generally open to the public except along a tour route. The regulations outline this case as follows:

> If a tour of a commercial facility that is not otherwise a place of public accommodation, such as, for example, a factory or a movie studio production set, is open to the general public, the route followed by the tour is a place of public accommodation and the tour must be operated in accordance with the rule's requirements for public accommodations. The place of public accommodation defined by the tour does not include those portions of the commercial facility that are merely viewed from the tour route. Hence, the barrier

removal requirements of Section 36.304 only apply to the physical route followed by the tour participants and not to work stations or other areas that are merely adjacent to, or within view of, the tour route. If the tour is not open to the general public, but rather is conducted, for example, for selected business colleagues, partners, customers, or consultants, the tour route is not a place of public accommodation and the tour is not subject to the requirements for public accommodation.

Another example of this might be an entity whose public contact is limited to the lobby, conference room, restrooms, and resource area while at the same time prohibiting public access to a secured private office area. Common sense would have you believe that the public areas should be required to meet the standard of Section 302 for the removal of existing architectural barriers while the secured private offices might require only altered portions to be accessible.

It is interesting to note the congressional development of the phrase **"commercial facilities"**. As can be seen in the following congressional report statement, the term "commercial facilities" was derived from the phrase **"potential places of employment"** and was altered to inhibit confusion between Title III and Title I:

> The phrase **"commercial facilities"** has been substituted for the phrase **"potential places of employment"** of HR2273 in order to eliminate any possible confusion between coverage of Title III concerning new construction and coverage of Title I concerning employment practices. Obviously, there is an intended conceptual connection between the two Titles. To the extent that new facilities are built in a manner that makes them accessible to all individuals including potential employees, there will be less of a need for individual entities to engage in reasonable accommodations for particular employees. The legal requirements of the two Titles, however, are separate and independent.

> The term **"commercial facilities"**, retains the same definition as that given to **"potential places of employment"** in the Senate Bill (S933). The new term, therefore, is designed solely to eliminate any unnecessary confusion regarding coverage of employees; it is not intended to reduce the scope of the definition (i.e., any facility intended for non-residential use). Further, the term is **not** intended to

be defined by dictionary or common industry definition. Rather "commercial facility" which is to be interpreted consistently with "potential places of employment" is defined as in S933, broadly, to include any facility that is intended for non-residential use and whose operations will affect commerce. Thus, for example, office buildings, factories and other places in which employment will occur come within this definition. The phrase "whose operations will affect commerce" is intended to include the full scope of coverage under federal constitutional commerce clause doctrine.

General Rule

The **general rule** pertaining to public accommodations in Title III of ADA is found is Section 302(a), and reads as follows:

> General Rule—No individual shall be discriminated against on the basis of disability in the full and equal enjoyment of the goods, services, facilities, privileges, advantages, or accommodations of any place of public accommodation by any person who owns, leases (or leases to), or operates a place of public accommodation.

It should be noted that this **general rule** is specifically targeting "public accommodations". It does **not** cover these buildings or portions of buildings defined as only "commercial facilities".

Participation in an Equal Manner

ADA mandates that the disabled have the opportunity to participate in or benefit from a "good, service, facility, privilege, advantage or accommodation" that is "equal" to that afforded to other individuals. The regulations state:

> Full and equal enjoyment means the right to participate and to have an equal opportunity to obtain the same results as others to the extent possible with such accommodations as may be required by the Act and these regulations. It does not mean that an individual with a disability must achieve an identical result or level of achievement as persons without a disability. For example, an exercise class cannot exclude a person who uses a wheelchair because he or she cannot do all of the exercises and derive the same result from the class as persons without a disability.

Segregation Concerns

ADA states that it is discriminatory to provide a person with disabilities with "a good, service, facility, privilege, advantage, or accommodation that is **different or separate from** that provided to other individuals, unless such action is necessary to provide the individual ... with a good, service, facility, privilege, advantage, or accommodation or other opportunity that is **as effective** as that provided to others".

With regard to **segregation,** the House Report from the Committee on Education and Labor states the following:

..... the Committee wishes to reaffirm that individuals with disabilities cannot be denied the opportunity to participate in programs that are not separate or different. This is an important and over-arching principal of the committee's bill. Separate, special or different programs that are designed to provide a benefit to persons with disabilities cannot be used in any way to restrict the participation of disabled persons in general integrated activities.

Providing services in the most integrated setting is a fundamental principal of the ADA. Historically, persons with disabilities have been relegated to separate and often inferior services. For example, seating for persons using wheelchairs is often located in the back of an auditorium. In addition to providing inferior seating, the patron in a wheelchair is forced to separate from family or friends during the performance.

The House Report continues, addressing issues of public safety and myths:

..... at times segregated seating is simply the result of thoughtlessness and indifference. At other times, safety concerns are raised, such as requiring the patrons to sit near theater exits because of perceived hazards in case of fire. The purported safety hazard is largely based on inaccurate assumptions and myths about the ability of people with disabilities to get around in such circumstances .....

A balance between the safety interest and the need to preserve a choice of seating for movie patrons who use wheelchairs has been accomplished under the existing Federal Accessibilities Standards (UFAS) that have applied since 1984 to theaters, auditoriums or other places of assembly constructed with federal funds.

These standards provide that wheelchair seating areas must be "dispersed throughout the seating area" and "located to provide lines of sight comparable for all viewing areas". Wheelchair areas are not restricted to areas "near an exit", but can be located at various parts of a theater so long as they "adjoin an accessible route that also serves as a means of egress in case of emergency". The availability of a choice of seating is critical to assure that patrons with disabilities are not **segregated** from family or friends.

The ADA Regulations offer the following examples of discrimination based upon the "integrated setting" rule: "For example, it would be a violation of this provision to require persons with disabilities to eat in the back room of a restaurant or to refuse to allow a person with a disability the full use of a health spa because of stereotypes about the persons ability to participate".

Roommate Clause

ADA states that it is discriminatory "to exclude or otherwise deny equal goods, services, facilities, privileges, advantages, accommodations, or other opportunities to an individuals or an entity because of a known disability of an individual with whom the individual or entity is known to have a **relationship or association**". The House Report from the Committee on Education and Labor suggests that the term "entity" as it's used in this section defines "..... entities that provide services to or are otherwise associated with people with disabilities .....". The same House Report suggests that examples of covered individuals or relationships that might fit under the "roommate clause" would be family members, spouses, friends, caretakers, and people who perform volunteer work for individuals who have disabilities. Others that might also fit under this umbrella might be dates, roommates, teammates, lovers, in-laws, co-workers, partners, employees, fellow religious worshippers, club members and the like. It might be well to note that the House Education and Labor Committee as well as the House Judicial Committee did not approve amendments that would have limited this designation to relatives "by blood, marriage, adoption, or guardianship". It is also interesting that a similar provision was included in the Fair Housing Amendments Act of 1988. These individuals with a relationship or association to a person with disabilities also have a right to file suit, if they believe themselves discriminated against.

Reasonable Modifications to Policies, Practices, and Procedures

The ADA states that an entity must make "**reasonable modifications in policies, practices or procedures** when such modifications are necessary to afford goods, services, privileges, advantages, or accommodations to individuals with disabilities unless the entity can demonstrate that making such modifications would fundamentally alter the nature of such goods, services, privileges, advantages, or accommodations". The House Report from the Committee on Education and Labor states that:

> .....it would also be a violation of this title to adopt policies which impose additional requirements or burdens upon people with disabilities that are not applied to other persons. Thus, it would be a violation for a theater or restaurant to adopt a policy specifying that individuals who use wheelchairs must be chaperoned by an attendant.

Another example would be if a private entity that operates a public parking garage refused to modify its policy of not allowing vans with raised roofs into the garage even if a person with a disability who had such a van could get to a parking space on the lowest level where head height was more than adequate. The regulations also state that it would be discriminatory for a hotel to give its last accessible room to someone other than the person with a disability who had made reservations for that night.

Auxiliary Aids and Services

The regulations state the following with regard to this topic:

> Section 36.303 of the final rule requires a public accommodation to take such steps as may be necessary to ensure that no individual with a disability is excluded, denied services, segregated or otherwise treated differently than other individuals because of the absence of auxiliary aids and services, unless the public accommodation can demonstrate that taking such steps would **fundamentally alter the nature** of the goods, services, facilities, advantages, **or** accommodations being offered or would result in an **undue burden**. This requirement is based on section 302(b)(2)(A)(iii) of the ADA.

> Implicit in this duty to provide auxiliary aids and services is the underlying obligation of a public accommodation to communicate effectively with its customers, clients, patients, or participants who have disabilities affecting hearing, vision, or speech.

Auxiliary aids and services are the part of the general mandate against discrimination of persons with disabilities that focuses on communication. The regulations give the following examples:

(b) Examples. The term "auxiliary aids and services" includes—

(1) Qualified interpreters, notetakers, computer-aided transcription services, written materials, telephone handset amplifiers, assistive listening devices, assistive listening systems, telephones compatible with hearing aids, closed caption decoders, open and closed captioning, telecommunications devices for deaf persons (TDD's), videotext displays, or other effective methods of making aurally delivered materials available to individuals with hearing impairments;

(2) Qualified readers, taped texts, audio recordings, Brailled materials, large print materials, or other effective methods of making visually delivered materials available to individuals with visual impairments;

(3) Acquisition or modification of equipment or devices; and

(4) Other similar services and actions.

(c) Effective communication. A public accommodation shall furnish appropriate auxiliary aids and services where necessary to ensure effective communication with individuals with disabilities.

The requirement above for TDD's is specifically called out for public accommodations who offer client, patients, or others an opportunity to make outgoing calls on "more than an incidental convenience basis" to make TDD's available upon request from a person with a hearing impairment.

In hotels or other places of lodging where TVs are provided in more than 5 guest rooms or patient rooms in hospitals, a "closed caption" decoder must be made available upon request.

What happens if a public accommodation believes provision of a particular auxiliary aid or service would be an undue burden or fundamentally alter it's services? The regulations shed light on this concern:

Alternatives. If provision of a particular auxiliary aid or service by a public accommodation would result in a fundamental alteration in the nature of the goods, services, facilities, privileges, advantages, or accommodations being offered or in an undue burden, i.e., significant difficulty or expense, the public accommodation shall provide an alternative auxiliary aid or service, if one exists, that would not result in an alteration or such burden but would nevertheless ensure that, to the maximum extent possible, individuals with disabilities receive the goods, services, facilities, privileges, advantages, or accommodations offered by the public accommodation.

Existing Facilities—Title III

Title III states that not only should existing public accommodations and commercial facilities construct alterations to existing buildings in an accessible manner, but private entities must remove "architectural and communication barriers" in places of public accommodation.

Removal of Architectural Barriers

The ADA requires the removal of **"architectural barriers"** that are structural in nature from existing public accommodations (not commercial facilities) where such removal is "readily achievable". The term "readily achievable" is that which is "easily accomplishable and able to be carried out without much difficulty or expense" The House Reports give examples of **architectural barriers** when they state,

> .....the kind of barrier removal which is envisioned, however, includes the addition of grab bars, the simple ramping of a few steps, the lowering of telephones, the addition of raised letters and Braille markings on elevator control buttons, the addition of flashing alarm lights and similar modest adjustments.

The ADA regulations offer the following examples, which appear to be an expansion upon the House Report list. Note that this list is not all-inclusive or limiting.

1. Installing ramps
2. Making curb cuts in sidewalks and entrances
3. Lowering shelves
4. Rearranging tables, chairs, vending machines, display racks and other furniture
5. Lowering telephones
6. Adding raised letters markings on elevator control buttons
7. Installing flashing alarm lights
8. Widening doors
9. Installing offset hinges to widen doorways

10. Eliminating a turnstile or providing an alternate accessible path
11. Installing accessible door hardware
12. Installing grab bars in toilet stalls
13. Rearranging toilet partitions to increase maneuvering space
14. Insulating lavatory pipes
15. Installing a raised toilet seat
16. Installing full length mirrors
17. Lowering the paper towel dispenser in a bath room
18. Creating a designated accessible parking space
19. Installing an accessible paper cup dispenser at an existing inaccessible water fountain
20. Removing high pile, low density carpeting
21. Modifying vehicle hand controls

The report continues, addressing furniture and equipment as follows:

> .....this section may require the removal of physical barriers including those created by the arrangement [or] location of such temporary or movable structures as furniture, equipment and display racks. For example, a restaurant may need to rearrange tables and chairs or a department store may need to adjust its layout of display racks and shelves, in order to permit access to individuals who use wheelchairs, where these actions can be carried out without much difficulty or expense.

> .....the Committee does not intend that a department store separate each and every display fixture in order to provide wheelchair clearance maneuverability. It is sufficient if a customer who uses a wheelchair is able to determine, once in a department, that the store offers, for example, black leather jackets. Once that is determined, the customer can rely upon a sales person to retrieve the black leather jacket in the customer's size.

Continuing, the Report addresses issues of more extensive and expensive alterations:

> A public accommodation would not be required to provide physical access if there is a flight of steps that would require extensive ramping or an elevator. The readily achievable standard only requires physical access that can be achieved without extensive restructuring or burdensome expense.

The standard, therefore, associated with **"readily achievable removal of architectural barriers"** is lower than that required by the new construction and alteration portions of Title III.

The regulations suggest that the removal of barriers be prioritized to 1) allow access and entry to the place of public accommodations, 2) provide access to the areas where goods and services are offered, 3) allow access to restrooms, and lastly, 4) comply with all other requirements of the law regarding the access to goods, services, facilities, etc. This will be covered in more depth in the chapter on compliance.

Barrier removal not done on or before January 26, 1992 opens a public accommodation up to possible discrimination suits. Accessment for barrier removal is also an on going responsibility for public accommodations.

The regulations state that when you elect to remove a barrier (that is "readily achievable") measures taken to modify the existing facility must be in compliance with the requirements of the ADA Accessibility Guidelines for alteration (except for the path of travel requirement). It states further:

> If, as a result of compliance with the alterations requirements specified in paragraph (d)(1) of this section, the measures required to remove a barrier would not be readily achievable, a public accommodation may take other readily achievable measures to remove the barrier that do not fully comply with the specified requirements. Such measures include, for example, providing a ramp with a steeper slope or widening a doorway to a narrower width than that mandated by the alterations requirements. No measure shall be taken, however, that poses a significant risk to the health or safety of individuals with disabilities or others.

Communication Barriers

The ADA requires the removal of "communication barriers" where such removable is "readily achievable". **Communication barriers,** as was mentioned before under architectural barriers, are elements of the building that do not allow for "communication" and might include the lack of raised letters or Braille markings at elevator control buttons, no flashing alarm lights, no tactile warnings on door knobs for blind individuals, and no curbs that might designate to the blind, using canes, that an obstruction is overhead. Although these are just a few of the elements that might constitute **"communication barriers"** we must look to the regulations issued by the Justice Department for more examples.

Alternative Methods

It is also important to know where an entity can show that the removal of a barrier is not "readily achievable", goods, services, facilities, privileges, advantages, or accommodations would be available through **"alternative methods"** if those methods are "readily achievable" also. The House Report elaborates on the issue of alternative methods as follows:

> With respect to the adoption of alternative methods, examples of "readily achievable" methods include: coming to the door to receive or return dry cleaning; allowing a disabled patron to be served beverages at a table even though non-disabled patrons having only drinks are required to drink at the inaccessible bar; providing assistance to retrieve items in an inaccessible location; and rotating movies from the first floor accessible theater and a comparable second floor inaccessible theater and notifying the public of the movies locations in advertisements.

The issue of "alternative methods" is addressed in a very similar way in the regulations distributed by the Department of Justice. The regulations also noted the following limitations:

> In some circumstances, because of security considerations, some alternative methods may not be readily achievable. The rule does not require a cashier to leave his or her post to retrieve items for individuals with disabilities, if there are no other employees on duty.

> **Personal Devices and Services**: This section does not require a public accommodation to provide its customers, clients, or participants with personal devices, such as wheelchairs, or services of a personal nature including assistance in eating, toileting or dressing.

> For example, if it is not readily achievable for a retail store to raise, lower, or remove shelves or to rearrange display racks to provide accessible aisles, the store must, if readily achievable, provide a clerk or take other alternative measures to retrieve inaccessible merchandise. Similarly, if it is not readily achievable to ramp a long flight of stairs leading to the front door

of a restaurant or a pharmacy, the restaurant or the pharmacy must take alternative measures, if readily achievable, such as providing curb service or home delivery. If, within a restaurant it is not readily achievable to remove physical barriers to a certain section of a restaurant, the restaurant must where it is readily achievable to do so, offer the same menu in an accessible area of the restaurant.

Where alternative methods are used to provide access, a public accommodation may not charge an individual with a disability for the costs associates with the alternative method (see section 36.301(c)).

Alteration Requirements

With regard to **alterations** to existing facilities, Section 303 of the law states that it is discriminatory to fail .....

..... to make alterations in such a manner that, to the maximum extent feasible, the altered portions of the facility are readily accessible to and usable by individuals with disabilities, including individuals who use wheelchairs. Where the entity is undertaking an alteration that affects or could affect usability of or access to an area of a facility containing a primary function, the entity shall also make the alterations in such a manner that to the maximum extent feasible, the path of travel to the altered area and the bathrooms, telephones, and drinking fountains serving the altered area, are readily accessible to and usable by individuals with disabilities where such alterations to the path of travel or the bathrooms, telephones, and drinking fountains serving the altered area are not disproportionate to the overall alteration in terms of cost and scope as determined under criteria established by the Attorney General.

Again, we find that the higher standard of **"readily accessible to and usable by"** the disabled is invoked on this issue of the law and that certain areas are noted as "primary function" areas and lastly, that a new term "disproportionate" is used when describing a limitation or cap on spending associated with modifications to the path of travel to an altered area. All of these issues will be addressed next in our review of other ADA concepts.

The regulations explain exactly when the alterations to existing facilities need to comply with the ADAAG:

... an alteration will be deemed to be undertaken after January 26, 1992 if the physical alterations of the property begins after that date. As a matter of interpretation, the Department (of Justice) will construe this provision to apply to alterations that require a permit from a state, county of local government, if physical alterations pursuant to the terms of the permit begin after January 26, 1992.

The Department recognizes that this application of the effective date may require redesign of some facilities that were planned prior to the publication of this part (regulations), but no retrofitting will be required of facilities on which the physical alterations were initiated prior to the effective date of the Act. Of course, nothing in this section in any way alters the obligation of any facility to remove architectural barriers in existing facilities to the extent that such barrier removal is readily achievable.

What does the term "usability" mean in relation to alterations? Again we turn to the regulations:

The Department remains convinced that the Act requires the concept of "usability" to be read broadly to include any change that effects the usability of the facility not simply changes that relate to access by individuals with disabilities.
... alterations include, but are not limited to, remodeling, renovations, rehabilitation, reconstruction, historic restoration, changes or rearrangement in structural parts of elements, and changes or rearrangement in the plan configuration of walls and full-height partitions. Normal maintenance, reroofing, painting or wall papering, asbestos removal, or changes to mechanical and electrical systems are not alterations unless they affect the "usability of (the) building or facility.

New Construction—Title III

Under Section 303 of ADA the law states that all new construction must be "**readily accessible to and usable by** individuals with disabilities except where an entity can demonstrate that it is structurally impracticable to meet the requirements .....". This requirement of ADA becomes effective if the new construction has its first occupancy on or after January 26, 1993.

The regulations really give the best description of the intent for ADA regarding new construction:

Potential patrons of places of public accommodation such as retail establishments, should be able to get to a store, get into the store and get to the areas where goods are being provided. Employees should have the same types of access, although those individuals require access to and around the employment areas as well as to the areas in which goods and services are provided.

The Act does not require new construction or alterations; it simply requires that when a public accommodation or other private entity undertakes the construction or alteration of a facility subject to the Act, the newly constructed or altered facility must be made accessible.

As stated above, all newly constructed or altered areas of facilities, either commercial facilities or public accommodations, must be accessible.

We discussed earlier the phrase **"readily accessible to and usable by"** is a greater standard than "readily achievable removal of architectural barriers" and will be the same standard adopted for alterations as well as new construction. To meet this standard for accessibility, new construction must be designed to comply with ADA (ADAAG) Accessible Guidelines.

Elevators—Title III

Although ADA does not require the installation of elevators in existing structures to meet the mandates of Section 302 (removal of architectural barriers), it does mandate that **elevators** installed in new construction and in alterations meet ADA Accessibility Guideline requirements with regard to controls, size of the cars, height of letters or numerals, floor identification, etc. In new construction and in alterations, all buildings (public accommodations and commercial facilities) having three or more floors of at least 3,000 square feet on any floor are required to have elevators. And elevators may be required in those new facilities that have less than 3,000 square feet of floor area if they contain healthcare provider offices, transportation terminals or retail facilities.

The Department of Justice elaborates further about the elevator exemption in Title III and the concept of "ready access" in the following excerpt from the regulations:

The elevator exemption is an exemption to the general requirements that new facilities be readily accessible to and usable by individuals with disabilities.

Generally, an elevator is the common way to provide individuals who use wheelchairs "ready access" to floor levels above or below the ground floors of a multi-story building.

In buildings eligible for the exemption, therefore, "ready access" from the building entrance to a floor above or below the ground floor is not required, because the statue does not require that an elevator be installed in such buildings.

This concept of an exemption to the "ready access" to floors above or below ground level really means that these facilities are exempt from providing an accessible route from one floor to the next. It really exempts a facility that is eligible from having to install an elevator, ramp, platform lift or any other means of vertical travel. For more information see the appendix of the ADAAG.

Key Supporting Concepts

In this portion of our overview of the ADA we will review the meaning of the terms "readily achievable", "undue burden", and "reasonable accommodation" along with the phrases "fundamental alterations", "readily accessible to and usable by", "structurally impracticable" and "disproportionate". Each of these terms or phrases plays a key role in understanding the basic anti- discriminatory requirements of Title III.

Readily Accessible To and Usable By

The phrase **"Readily accessible to and usable by"** individuals with disabilities establishes the standard by which that new construction and alteration project would be judged.

This legal term has been previously used in the Architectural Barriers Act of 1968, the Fair Housing Amendments Act of 1988, Regulations in Section 504 of the Rehabilitation Act of 1973 and the Uniform Federal Accessibility Standards. The essence of this term or phrase might be clear if we review the congressional committee reports which say the following:

> The term is intended to enable people with disabilities (including mobility, sensory, and cognitive impairments) to get to, enter, and use a facility. While the term does not necessarily require accessibility of every part of every area of a facility, the term contemplates a high degree of convenient accessibility, entailing accessibility of parking areas, accessible routes to and from the facility, accessible entrances, usable

bathrooms and water fountains, accessibility of public and common use areas, and access to the goods, services, programs, facilities, accommodations and work areas available at the facility.

The ADA regulations state that new facilities and alterations that are constructed to meet the requirements of the ADA Accessibility Guidelines will be considered "readily accessible and usable" with respect to construction.

The congressional reports also include a discussion to help limit confusion over similar terms such as **"readily accessible"** and **"readily achievable".**

The concept of readily achievable should not be confused with term "readily accessible" used in regard to accessibility requirements for alterations and new construction (Section 303). While the word "readily" appears in both phrases and has roughly the same meaning in each context, i.e., easily, without much difficulty, the concepts of "readily achievable" and "readily accessible" are sharply distinguishable and almost polar opposites in focus.

The phrase **"readily accessible to and usable by** individuals with disabilities" focuses on the person with a disability and addresses the degree of ease with which such an individual can enter and use a facility; it is access and useability which must be "ready".

"Readily achievable", on the other hand, focuses on the business operator and addresses the degree of ease of difficulty of the business operator in the removing a barrier; if barrier-removal cannot be accomplished readily, then it is not required.

What the "readily achievable" standard will mean in any particular public accommodation will depend on the circumstances, considering the factors listed previously.

The term is not intended to require that all parking spaces, bathrooms, stalls within bathrooms, etc. are accessible; only a reasonable number must be accessible depending upon such factors as their use, location, and number. However, when the facilities involved do not serve identical functions, each facility must be accessible. For example, meeting rooms at a conference center may be used for different purposes at any given time and therefore all must be accessible. Accessibility elements for each particular type of facility should assure both ready access to the facility, useability of its features or equipment, and of goods, services and programs available within.

The congressional report continues by giving an example of a physician's office and of those areas within the office that should be **"readily accessible to and usable by"** those with disabilities.

> In a physician's office, "readily accessible to and usable by" would include ready access to the waiting areas, the bathroom, and a percentage of the examining rooms.

It is interesting to note that Congress has tied Title III, which deals with public accommodations, to Title I, concerning employment issues of ADA, through, among other things, the standard of **"readily accessible to and usable by"**. A Congressional Report reads as follows:

> As noted above, the standard of **"readily accessible to and usable by"** applies not only to areas that will be used by patrons, (public accommodations) but also to areas that may be used by disabled employees. The parameters of the standard as it applies to patrons has been set forth above. The same basic approach applies in employment areas for both public accommodations and commercial facilities. Thus access into and out of the rooms is required. In addition, there must be an accessible path of travel in and around the employment area. The basic objective is that a person with a disability must be able to get to the employment area. The design standards do not cover unusual areas such as catwalks or fan rooms.

With regard to **new construction** and **alterations** as required under Section 303, the Congressional Reports speak to the issues of **furnishings** and **fixtures** as follows:

> The standard does not require, however, that individual work stations be constructed accessible or be outfitted with fixtures that make it accessible to a person with a disability. Such modifications will come into play in the form of **"reasonable accommodations"** when a person with a disability applies for a specific job and is governed by the "undue hardship" standard. If the builder builds fixtures and equipment to service a work site (e.g., racks, shelves), the fixtures and

shelves do not have to be made accessible. If a qualified person with a disability applies, whether such fixtures and equipment can be modified to allow the person to do the job would be an issue of "reasonable accommodation".

Two items regarding the placement of fixtures and equipment should be noted. As has often been pointed out, it is always **less expensive** to build something new in an accessible manner than it is to retrofit an existing area to make it accessible. That concept applies as well in the building and placement of fixtures and equipment. Thus, if it would not affect the useability or enjoyment by members of the general public, consideration should be given in new construction to placing fixtures and equipment at a convenient height for accessibility. In addition, if they are commercially available and it would not affect useability or enjoyment by the general public, an effort should be made to purchase new fixtures and equipment that are adjustable so that reasonable accommodations in the future may not pose undue hardships.

Readily Achievable

The term **"readily achievable"** is a new statutory phrase utilized in ADA. It comes into play under the alterations rule of the "architectural barriers" portion of Section 302 of the general rules of discrimination in public accommodations. The law states that it's unlawful not to remove architectural and communication barriers from existing facilities if such removal is **"readily achievable"**. It's important to note that this term should not be misunderstood or seen in the same light as the phrase "readily accessible". The law defines **"readily achievable"** as follows:

The term "readily achievable" means easily accomplishable and able to be carried out without much difficulty or expense. In determining whether an action is readily achievable, factors to be considered include the following: (a) the nature and cost of the action needed under this act; (b) the overall financial resources of the facility or facilities involved in this action, the number of persons employed at such facility, the affect on expenses and resources or the impact otherwise of such action upon the operation of the facility; (c) the overall financial resources of the covered entity, the overall size of the business of the covered entity with respect to the number of its employees, the number, type, and location of its facilities; and (d) the type of operation or operations of the covered entity, including the composition, structure, and function of the work force of such entity, the geographic separateness, administrative or fiscal responsibility of the facility or facilities in question to the covered entity.

It seems that it was a rigorous decision making process for Congress to choose which **"standard of care"** should be followed when addressing the removal of architectural and communication barriers from existing facilities. The following is an excerpt from the Congressional Report on ADA:

> The Committee was faced with a choice in how to address the question of what actions, if any, a public accommodation should be required to take in order to remove structural barriers in existing facilities and vehicles. On one hand, the Committee could have required retrofitting of all existing facilities and vehicles to make them fully accessible. On the other hand, the Committee could have required that no actions be required to be taken to remove barriers in existing facilities and vehicles.

The Committee rejected both of these alternatives and instead decided to adopt a modest requirement that public accommodations make structural changes or adopt alternative methods that are "readily achievable". It is important to note that **"readily achievable"** is a significantly lesser or lower standard than the **"undue burden"** used in this title and under the "undue hardship" standard used in Title I of this legislation. Any changes that are not easily accomplishable and are not able to be carried out without much difficulty or expense when the preceding factors are weighed, are not required under the "readily achievable" standard, even if they do not impose an undue burden."

It should be noted that the term **"undue burden"** that is spoken of in the Congressional Report quoted above, is taken from the 3rd paragraph under specific prohibitions in Section 302 of the law. This paragraph states essentially that auxiliary aids and services must be provided to individuals with disabilities where required unless taking such steps would fundamentally alter the good or service or would result in an **"undue burden"**.

The Congressional Report continues with regard to the **"readily achievable"** standard when they say the following:

Readily achievable ..... focuses on the business operator and addresses the degree of ease or difficulty of
the business operator in removing a barrier; if barrier
removal cannot be accomplished readily, then it is not
required.

What the "readily achievable" standard will mean in
any particular public accommodation will depend
upon the circumstances, considering the factors listed
previously. The kind of barrier removal which is
envisioned, however, includes the addition of grab
bars, the simple ramping of a few steps, the lowering
of telephones, the addition of raised letter and Braille
markings on elevator control buttons, the addition of
flashing alarm lights and similar modest adjustments.

This section may require the removal of physical barriers including those created by the arrangement or
location of such temporary or movable structures as
furniture, equipment and display racks. For example,
a restaurant may need to rearrange tables and chairs
or a department store may need to adjust its layouts
of display racks and shelves in order to permit access
to individuals who use wheelchairs where these actions can be carried out without much difficulty or
expense.

Even though restaurants might need to rearrange chairs and
tables if readily achievable, they are not required to take such
action if it "would result in a significant loss of selling or serving
space", as the regulations state. If it were to result in such a
loss, then it certainly would not be "readily achievable". In that
case another method of barrier removal would be required as
long as it was "readily achievable".

The intention seems clear from the above Congressional Report
that **"readily achievable"** does, in fact, mean without much
difficulty or expense. Therefore, the removal of architectural
barriers under Section 302 will need to be considered on a case
by case basis, taking into account all of the factors mentioned in
the definition of the term "readily achievable", i.e., nature and
cost of the action, overall financial resources of the facilities, etc.
This is reinforced by the Committee Report which states:

This readily achievable analysis must be done on a
case by case basis. The Committee cannot give a
blanket statement of which specific actions are readily
achievable and thus required by this section. The

readily achievable standard provides flexibility for public accommodations to remove barriers and provide access for persons with disabilities.

Again, if the alterations or the removal of readily achievable architectural barriers is not easy or inexpensive, then service must be provided in an alternative manner, if that alternative manner is also readily achievable.

With regard to the term "readily achievable", the Judiciary Committee Report reinforces the idea mentioned above, that if "significant loss" of business opportunities would jeopardize the very existence of a business, the court should consider that when deciding what is "readily achievable".

In adopting this amendment, the Committee has responded to concerns about public accommodations that operate in depressed or rural areas that may be operating at the margin or at a loss. Specifically, concern was expressed that a business may close a site if it is losing money rather than undertaking significant investments to remove barriers to allow access and use for persons with disabilities.

The Committee does not intend for the requirements of the Act to result in the closure of neighborhood stores or in the loss of jobs. Rather, the Committee intends for courts to consider as a factor in determining whether the removal of a barrier is 'readily achievable' whether the local store is threatened by closure by a parent company or is faced with job loss as a result of the requirements of this Act.

It is imperative that you understand the requirement for the readily achievable removal of architectural and communication barriers is an "on going" requirement. The regulations elaborate on this as follows:

The obligation to engage in readily achievable barrier removal is a continuing one. Over time, barrier removal that initially was not readily achievable may later be required because of changed circumstances.

Examples of what might be "readily achievable" include the list given earlier in this chapter under the Barrier Removal section. The Department of Justice gives more examples in the regulations:

A public accommodation generally would not be required to remove a barrier to physical access posed by a flight of steps, if removal would require extensive ramping or an elevator. Ramping a single step, however, will likely be readily achievable and ramping several steps will in many circumstances also be readily achievable. The readily achievable standard does not require barrier removal that requires extensive restructuring or burdensome expense. Thus, where it is not readily achievable to do, the ADA would not require a restaurant to provide access to a restroom reachable only by a flight of stairs.

For example, if it is not readily achievable for a retail store to raise, lower or remove shelves or to rearrange display racks to provide accessible aisles, the store must, if readily achievable, provide a clerk or take other alternative measures to retrieve inaccessible merchandise. Similarly, if it is not readily achievable to ramp a long flight of stairs leading to the front door of a restaurant or a pharmacy, the restaurant or the pharmacy must take alternative measures, if readily achievable, such as providing curb service or home delivery.

In considering whether a barrier removal is "readily achievable" there are a few factors to take into account. The following concerns are outlined by the Department of Justice:

1. The nature and cost of the action needed;

2. The overall financial resources of the site or sites involved in the action; the number of persons employed at the site; the effect on expenses and resources; legitimate safety requirements that are necessary for safe operation, including crime prevention measures; or the impact otherwise of the action upon the operation of the site;

3. The geographic separateness, and the administrative or fiscal relationship of the site or sites in questions to any parent corporation or entity;

4. If applicable, the overall financial resources of any parent corporation or entity; the overall size of the parent corporation or entity with respect to the number of its employees; the number, type, and location of its facilities; and

5. If applicable, the type of operation or operations of any parent corporation or entity, including the composition, structure and functions of the workforce of the parent corporation or entity.

What exactly is required of a parent corporation with regard to its responsibility to assist a specific site with readily achievable barrier removal? For more information we go again to the remarks of the Department of Justice:

The Department believes that this complex issue is most appropriately resolved on a case-by-case basis .... there is a wide variety of possible relationships between the site in question and any parent corporation or other entity. It would be unwise to posit legal ramifications under ADA of even generic relationships (e.g., banks involved in foreclosures or insurance companies operating as trustees or in other similar fiduciary relationships), because any analysis will depend so completely on the detailed fact situations and the exact nature of the legal relationships involved.

Although some commenters (on the proposed ADA regulations) sought more specific numerical guidance on the definition of readily achievable, the Department has declined to establish in the final rule any kind of numerical formula for determining what is readily achievable. It would be difficult to devise a specific ceiling on compliance costs that would take into account the vast diversity of enterprises covered by ADA's public accommodation requirements and the economic situation that any particular entity would fine itself in at any moment. The final rule, therefore, implements the flexible case-by-case approach charges by Congress.

To the Maximum Extent Feasible

The regulations offer the following insight for this concept:

The phrase "to the maximum extent feasible" as used in this section, applies to the occasional case where the nature of an existing facility makes it impossible to comply fully with applicable accessibility standards through a plan alteration. In these circumstances, the alteration shall provide the maximum physical accessibility feasible. Any altered features of the facility or portion of the facility that can be made accessible shall be made accessible. If providing accessibility and conformance with this section to individuals with certain disabilities (eg. those who use wheelchairs) would not be feasible, the facility shall be made accessible to persons with other types of disabilities (eg. those who use crutches, those who have impaired vision or hearing, or those who have other impairments).

Undue Burden

We see in Section 302(2) which deals with the requirement for an entity to provide auxiliary aids and services unless it can be demonstrated that taking such steps would **fundamentally alter** the nature of the goods, services, facility, privilege, advantage or accommodation being offered, or secondly, if providing the auxiliary aids and services would be an **"undue burden"**. The House Report from the Committee on Education and Labor states the following:

> The determination of whether the provision of an auxiliary aid or service imposes an undue burden on a business will be made on a case by case basis taking into account the same factors used for purposes of determining undue hardship (see Title I concerns).

The fact that the provision of a particular auxiliary aid will result in an undue burden does not relieve the business from the duty to furnish an alternate auxiliary aid, if available, that would not result in such a burden.

Under Title I, Section 101, the definition of **"undue hardship"** is "an action requiring significant difficulty or expense when considered in light of the factors set forth in Subparagraph B" which include:

1. the nature and cost of the accommodation;

2. the overall financial resources and work force of the facility involved;

3. the overall financial resources, number of employees, and structure of the parent entity; and

4. the type of operations of the covered entity including the composition and functions of its work force and the administrative and physical relationships between the facility and the parent entity.

It seems very clear that Congress had, as its intent, to focus on the needed accommodations and the impact that the accommodation would have on a particular business rather than a lump sum dollar figure or arbitrary formula. It should also be noted that the House defeated in a floor vote an amendment that suggested the proposed accommodation would be an **"undue hardship"** if its cost exceeded 10% of the annual salary of the person for whom the accommodation was to be made. This action suggests that the House thought that the 10% of annual salary interpretation for "undue hardship" was too restrictive a standard for ADA.

Disproportionate to Overall Alterations

This phrase is found in Section 303 dealing with alterations to existing facilities. The law states that **alterations** to existing facilities are to the maximum extent feasible **readily accessible to and usable by** those with disabilities and further states that the path of travel to the altered portion of the existing facility may or may not be required to be renovated so as to become readily accessible to and usable by those with disabilities. The guidelines governing the requirement that the path of travel to and/or from the altered portion of an existing facility have been defined in the Justice Department regulations but may also rely upon information presented in Congressional hearings for a clue as to the decision to make these paths accessible or not. A Congressional Report states the following:

> Where the entity is undertaking an alteration or could effect the usability or access to an area of the facility containing a **primary function,** the entity must also make the alterations in such a manner, to the maximum extent feasible, that the path of travel to the area, and the bathrooms, telephones, and drinking fountains serving the remodeled area, are readily accessible to and usable by individuals with disabilities, where such alterations to the path of travel or the bathrooms, telephones, and drinking fountain serving the altered area are not **"disproportionate"** to the overall alteration in terms of cost and scope (as determined under the criteria established by the Attorney General).

> Under the language of Section 302(b)(2)(A)(vi), an "alteration that affects or could affect usability of or access to an area of the facility concerning a **primary function**" triggers an obligation to provide an accessible path of travel to the altered area, and to make bathrooms, telephones and drinking fountains serving the altered area accessible. That such alterations must or could affect usability means that minor changes such as painting or wallpapering, replacing ceiling tiles, or similar alterations that do not affect useability or access do not trigger the requirement

that the altered area must be made accessible or that the path of travel in bathrooms and other facilities must be made accessible.

Areas containing **primary functions** refer to those portions of a facility where the major activities for which that facility was designed are housed. A mechanical room, boiler room, supply storage room, or janitorial closet is clearly not an area containing a primary function; the customer service lobby of a bank, the dining area of a cafeteria, the meeting rooms in a conference center, the viewing galleries of a museum as well as offices and other work areas of a public accommodation or private entities are areas containing a **primary function.**

The regulations offer another example of a "primary function" space by stating:

> For example, the availability of public restrooms at a place of public accommodation at a roadside rest stop may be a major factor affecting customers' decisions to patronize the public accommodation. In that case, a restroom would be considered to be an "area containing a primary function" of the facility.

It is required that when primary function areas of a facility are altered in a manner that affects or could affect the useability or accessibility of the area, an accessible path of travel as well as restrooms, telephones, and drinking fountains serving the altered area must be made accessible, if doing so would not be **"disproportionate** in terms of cost and scope of the overall alterations". This language sets out an expectation that an accessible path of travel and accessible facilities should generally be included when alterations are done to primary function areas, unless achieving such accessibility would be out of proportion with the overall alterations being undertaken. Examples of alterations to "primary function" areas that affect usability include, but are not limited to:

1. Remodeling merchandise display areas or employee work areas in a department store;

2. Replacing an inaccessible floor surface in the customer service area or employee work areas of a bank;

3. Redesigning the assembly line area of a factory; or

4. Installing a computer center in an accounting firm.

Examples of alterations not triggering "path of travel" requirements include alterations to hardware, windows, electrical outlets and signage as these don't affect the "usability" of or access to a "primary function" space.

The **disproportionality concept** "recognizes that in some circumstances achieving an accessible path of travel and accessible restrooms and drinking fountains may be sufficiently significant in terms of cost or scope in comparison to the remainder of the rest of the alterations being undertaken as to render this requirement unreasonable. In such cases where the tail (path of travel, accessible restrooms, etc.) would be wagging the dog (the overall alteration), the accessible path of travel and related accessibility features are **not** required".

> Of course a place of public accommodations may not evade the path of travel, accessible restrooms, etc., requirements by performing a series of small alterations which it would otherwise have performed in a single undertaking. The committee notes that in Pennsylvania, a state statute requires that any series of alterations projects on a facility conducted within three years is combined as if they were a single alteration for the purposes of determining the extent of accessibility requirements. Likewise, under ADA, if a public accommodation has completed an alteration without incorporating the accessible path of travel and accessible restrooms, etc., the total cost of the alterations both past and future which are proximate in time may appropriately be considered in determining whether providing an accessible path of travel, etc. is **"disproportionate"**.

The Committee Report continues addressing the issue of disproportionality and focuses next upon the issue of **phasing** portions of the accessibility work to the path of travel. The Committee Report continues as follows:

> If the aggregate cost of an accessible path of travel, restrooms, telephones and drinking fountains would be **disproportionate** to the overall alteration cost, the place of public accommodation is not relieved of the obligation to provide a "subset" of such features that is not disproportionate. The goal is to provide a maximum degree of accessibility in such features without exceeding the disproportionate limit. If a selection must be made between accessibility features, those which provide the greatest use of the facility should be selected. For example, an accessible entrance would generally be the most important path of travel feature

since without it the facility is totally unusable by many persons with disabilities. An accessible restroom would have a greater priority than an accessible drinking fountain.

In the comments above, we saw the intent of Congress to **prioritize** elements of the accessible path of travel in an area of alterations. What we find next is that even though the complete path of travel may not be made accessible, the entities are required to at least reach this magical "disproportionate limit" which will be discussed further in the Congressional Report quoted below:

> If there is no way to provide an accessible path of travel to an altered area because of the **disproportionality** limit, making restrooms, etc., serving the area accessible is still required if it is not disproportionate. It is incorrect to assume that if a building entrance has steps, there is no reason to make the restrooms and other features accessible. Some individuals with disabilities can negotiate steps but still need accessibility features in the restroom, drinking fountains, etc. If those contemplating alterations to places of public accommodations are unsure how to rank such accessibility features in particular circumstances, they would be well advised to consult with local organizations representing persons with disabilities.

As Congress mentioned in the report quoted above, if the priorities are unclear, consultation with local disability advocacy groups would be wise. This might also be incorporated into an "implementation" plan for accessibility which represents a **"good faith effort"** on the part of your company or organization. Congress did make their intent clear in the discussion that follows, as to what this magical **"disproportionate limit"** might be:

> For example, it would clearly be **disproportionate** to require a public accommodation to double the cost of a planned alteration. Indeed the Committee believes that, in almost all circumstances, it would be disproportionate to increase the cost of an alteration by more than 50% to incorporate an accessible path of travel and related accessibility features. The Committee notes that Pennsylvania statutes incorporate a formula in which an accessible path of travel is mandated whenever an alteration project costs between

30% and 50% of the worth of the building and the entire building must be made accessible if remodeling exceeds 50% of the building's value.

Although the language in the Committee Report is not necessarily the same as that which will be provided by the Department of Justice in their final regulations on this topic, the Justice Department representatives suggest that deviation from the intent expressed by Congress is extremely rare and requires stringent justification. The Congressional Report continues as follows:

> This (the Pennsylvania) approach differs somewhat from that in the ADA, in that the latter comprises the proportionality of the accessibility costs to the overall planned alteration rather than the underlying value of the building. The Committee believes, however, that it would be consistent with the ADA approach for the minimum guidelines or regulations to establish a specific standard, **such as 30%** of the alteration cost, for determining the **disproportionality** of the accessible path of travel in related accessibility features required under this Section 302.

This "magic" number for the **disproportionate limit** has been defined by the Justice Department to be **20%** (not 30%) of the alteration cost. This 20% limit or cap on "path of travel" expenditures is very important because alterations made to provide a more accessible path of travel are not required to exceed 20% of the "overall alteration" costs for the primary function area. If your modifications would require you to exceed this 20% limit, you should reconsider your modification strategies until you can make the "path of travel" as accessible as possible given the 20% cap on spending.

Also, a private entity can't try to evade the "path of travel" accessibility modifications by making a series of small alterations to the primary function area in a way that no significant amount of money is available to modify the "path of travel". In such a case, the 20% limit will be calculated using the sum of the alteration costs to that "primary function" area over the preceding three years.

The Congressional Report continues with a discussion on the definition **"path of travel"**:

> The **"path of travel"** to an altered area means a continuous, unobstructed way of pedestrian travel by means of which that area may be approached, entered, used, and exited; and which connects that area with

an exterior approach (including sidewalks, streets, and parking areas), and entrance to the facility, and other parts of the facility. An accessible path of travel may consist of walks and sidewalks, curb ramps, and other interior and exterior pedestrian ramps; clear floor paths through lobbies, corridors, rooms and other improved areas; parking area access aisles; elevators and lifts; or a combination of such elements. An accessible path of travel is analogous to the **"accessible route"** and **"circulation path"** concepts in the existing Uniform Federal Accessibility Standards.

Cost associated with making a path of travel more accessible might include those costs associated with:

1. Providing an accessible entrance and an accessible route to the altered areas (i.e., widening doors, installing ramps, or accessible door hardware).

2. Making restrooms more accessible (i.e., putting in grab bars, enlarging toilet stalls, insulating lavatory pipes, or installing lever handle faucets).

3. Providing accessible phones (i.e., lowering phones, installing adjustable volume receivers or TDD's).

4. Relocating drinking fountains.

In prioritizing how to spend the 20% for path of travel improvements, rank choices as follows:

1. Entrance accessibility;

2. Accessible route to altered areas;

3. At least one accessible restroom for each sex or a unisex restroom;

4. Telephones;

5. Miscellaneous improvements including parking, storage or alarms.

Fundamentally Alter the Nature of a Service

"Undue burden" is the first of two exemptions allowed in ADA under which a public accommodation may not be required to make auxiliary aids or services to people with disabilities to ensure communication. The second exemption occurs if those modifications might **"fundamentally alter"** the nature of the goods, service, facilities, privilege, advantage or accommodation being offered. This limitation or defense also holds true for discrimination based on the failure to modify policies, practices or procedures. This term, **"fundamental alterations"**, has yet to be defined by the ADA, the Supreme Court or in Section 504, Regulations of the Rehabilitation Act of 1973. Some lower courts have, in fact, addressed portions of the concept.

Courts have ruled that alterations are not required if they would endanger a program's viability, or if massive changes are required, or if modifications involve "major restructuring" of an enterprise or that "jeopardize the effectiveness" of a program or if they might alter an enterprise so as to create, in effect, a new program. In an article written by Bergdorf and Bell entitled Eliminating Discrimination Against Physically and Mentally Handicapped Persons; A Statutory Blueprint, "fundamental alteration" was defined as:

1. A substantial change in the primary purpose or benefit of a program or activity; or

2. A substantial impairment of necessary or essential components required to achieve a program or activity's primary purpose or activity.

Two simple examples are given in the regulations that help us to understand the concept of "fundamental alteration". The first is the case where a physician is forced to accept patients outside his or her specialty. This, the regulations say, is not required because it would "fundamentally alter the nature of the medical practice". The second example states that touching artwork in a museum in an attempt to understand the nature of a statue by those who have visual impairments could clearly alter the fundamental nature of the artwork if touching it would threaten the integrity of the piece or possibly damage it.

Again, **"Fundamental Alterations"** and **"Undue Burdens"** together comprise the limit of duty on public accommodations with regard to either "reasonable modifications" to policies, practices, and procedures, or the issues surrounding the provision of "auxiliary aids and services" of Section 302.

Structurally Impracticable

Under Title III, Section 303 dealing with new construction and alterations in public accommodations or commercial facilities, we find the term **"structurally impracticable"**. This term is used as an **exception** to the requirement that all new construction be "readily accessible to and usable by" individuals with disabilities. The House Report from the Committee on Education and Labor has the following to say with regard to **"structurally impracticable"**:

The phrase **"structurally impracticable"** is a narrow exception that will apply only in rare and unusual circumstances where unique characteristics of terrain make accessibility unusually difficult. Since limitations for topographical problems are analogous to an acknowledged limitation in the application of accessibility requirements of the Fair Housing Act of 1988. In the House Committee report accompanying the act, the House Committee of the Judicial noted:

Certain natural terrain may pose unique building problems. For example, in areas which flood frequently such as water fronts or marshlands, housing may traditionally be built on stilts. The committee does not intend to require that the accessibility requirements of this act override the act to protect the physical integrity of multi-family housing that may be built on such stilts.

By incorporating **"structurally impracticable",** this Title explicitly recognizes an exception analogous to the "physical integrity" exception of peculiarities of terrain recognized implicitly in the statutory language and expressly in the House Committee Report accompanying the Fair Housing Amendments Act. As under the Fair Housing Amendments Act this is intended to be a narrow exception to the requirement of accessibility. It means that only where unique characteristics of terrain prevent the incorporation of accessibility and would destroy the physical integrity of the facility is it acceptable to deviate from accessibility requirements. Buildings that must be built on stilts because of their locations in marshlands or over water are one of few situations in which structurally impracticable exceptions would apply.

Neither under this Title nor under the Fair Housing Amendment Act should an exception to accessibility requirements be applied to situations in which a facility is located in "hilly terrain or on a plot of land upon which there are steep grades". In such circumstances, accessibility can be achieved without destroying the physical integrity of the structure, and ought to be required in the construction of new facilities.

In these circumstances in which it is structurally impracticable to achieve full compliance with accessibility requirements of the ADA, public accommodations and commercial facilities should still be designed and constructed to incorporate accessibility features to the extent that they are structurally practicable. The accessibility requirement should not be viewed as an all-or-nothing proposition in such circumstances.

The Congressional Report continues with regard to this term and suggests that even if the facility in its entirety cannot be made readily accessible to and usable by people with disabilities, then those portions that can be made accessible should be made accessible to those with disabilities. Even if the facilities are exempted under the exception of "structurally impracticable", then they should be designed to accommodate those accessibility features to which the disabled will still have access.

An example was given in the report of a building built on stilts that was not accessible to those in wheelchairs. It is required under ADA that the building still be made readily accessible to and usable by those individuals with hearing and vision impairments and any other disability group that still has access to that facility.

Employee Work Stations

Work stations are of particular importance to those in the business community as they are becoming standard and have almost replaced the free standing desk in most "open-office" layouts.

The ADA regulations require that all areas "that may be used by employees with disabilities" must be designed and constructed so people with disabilities can "approach, enter and exit the areas". This is very important, because although not all individual work stations are required to be accessible, it does state that consideration shall be given to "the purchase and installation of commercially available fixtures and equipment accommodations to employees who will use the facility will not pose undue hardships." It is also required that those areas for general use by employees, but not the public, (such as restrooms, employee lounges, employee cafeterias, gyms, and health facilities) must be accessible.

Reasonable Accommodation

The Supreme Court has a history of using the terms "reasonable accommodations", "reasonable modifications" and "reasonable adjustments" interchangeably. Under Title III of ADA, the term "reasonable modifications" is used in Section 302 which prohibits acts of discrimination by places of public accommodation through failure to make "reasonable modifications" in policies, practices, or procedures when those modifications are necessary to allow disabled individuals access to goods, services, facilities, privileges, advantages, or accommodations, unless the entity can demonstrate that making those modifications would fundamentally alter the nature of that good, service, facility, privilege, advantage, or accommodation. ADA, using the employment perspective, defines **reasonable accommodation** as the following:

> The term "reasonable accommodation" may include: (a) making existing facilities used by employees readily accessible to and usable by individuals with disabilities; (b) job restructuring, part time or modifying the work, scheduling, reassignment to a vacant position, acquisition or modification of equipment or devices, appropriate adjustment or modifications of examinations, training materials or policies, the provision of qualified readers or interpreters, and other similar accommodations for individuals with disabilities.

It is interesting to note that the U.S. Commission on Civil Rights attempted to redefine the term **"reasonable accommodations"** to mean the following:

> Providing or modifying devices, services, or facilities or changing practices or procedures in order to match a particular person with a particular program or activity. Individualizing opportunities is this definition's essence.

Although ADA follows the intent of the Commissions' definition, it did not elect to utilize that definition. Also in the House Judiciary Committee Report, it was stated that the reasonable accommodations requirement is "central to the non-discrimination mandate of the ADA" and also **"a reasonable accommodation** should be tailored to the needs of the individual and the requirements of the job". Further guidance can be drawn from the House Education and Labor Committee which states:

> The Committee believes that the reasonable accommodation requirement is best understood as a process in which barriers to a particular individual's equal employment opportunity are removed. The accommodation process focuses on the need of a particular individual in relation to problems in performance of a particular job because of physical or mental impairment. A problem solving approach should be used to identify the particular tasks or aspects of the work environment that limit performance and to

identify possible accommodations that will result in a meaningful equal opportunity for the individual with the disability.

The Committee suggests that after a request for an accommodation has been made, employers first will consult with and involve the individual with a disability in deciding on the appropriate accommodation.

For more information on this area of **"reasonable modification"** or **"reasonable accommodation"** review the regulations issued by the Equal Employment Opportunity Commission.

*   *   *

Accessibility Guidelines

Accessible design has been an issue that many Architects and Planners have "glossed over" for many, many years. The essence of the issue is very simple—**provide access for those who are disabled.** The reality of making a facility accessible to those with disabilities is another question entirely. This question involves site conditions, building layout, facility size, cost, functional planning and aesthetic concerns just to name a few.

Accessibility Standards such ANSI A117.1 and the Uniform Federal Accessibility Standards have been available for many years, but depending upon the owner of the project, the municipality responsible for approving the design and inspecting that project, the legal requirement for providing accessible buildings may or may not have been in place. Some municipalities have not adopted accessibility standards or have not adopted ordinances requiring the facilities to be built in an accessible manner.

With the passage of the American's with Disabilities Act of 1990, the issue of municipalities being required to pass an ordinance mandating accessibility is of little consequence. The Federal Government now mandates that nearly all new buildings must be accessible to and usable by the disabled. As was mentioned in our review of the law, the Architectural and Transportation Barriers Compliance Board (ATBCB) has provided guidelines (ADA Accessibility Guidelines) by which the design of facilities covered by this law is to be judged. What follows is an overview of those accessibility issues that each of us must review in our own facilities to ensure that they comply with the ADA.

Although, as was mentioned above, the essence of the ADA is to prevent discrimination against people with disabilities, your **primary concerns** should probably be: arriving at a strategy for surveying your existing facilities, analyzing the requirements of ADA, identifying potential accessibility problems within your existing facilities, prioritizing corrective work, having your Architect prepare construction documents for the corrective work, and then constructing the modifications required to provide your facility with the accessibility level mandated under the law. Keep in mind that your risk of civil suit increases dramatically if the corrective work to existing facilities has not been completed by **January 26, 1992.**

Along these same lines, you should instruct your Architects to incorporate the accessible design requirements of the law in all **new facilities** or **alterations** that you plan in the future.

Included in this review will be issues such as site concerns, building approach concerns, interior accessibility concerns, and special occupancy concerns. As the ADA Accessibility Guidelines have just been published (Federal Register—July 26, 1991) there is where we will focus our attention with regard to accessibility requirements. This book should not be substituted for ADAAG or any other legally mandated guideline or regulation but should be viewed as a tool for a greater understanding of some of the elements in the ADA (ADAAG) Accessibility Guidelines. Refer to the ADAAG as you review this chapter since all of the illustrations referenced herein are those drawings in the ADAAG. Consider this chapter a "tour" through the ADAAG. We will go through some of the most important issues. Then we will break down the guidelines into two primary areas, Exterior Accessible Route issues and Interior Accessible Route issues.

Accessible Route

As you begin to learn about issues associated with accessible design, you will benefit from subdividing accessibility issues into two broad, yet understandable categories—exterior accessibility issues, and interior accessibility issues—and your overall concern should be on understanding how someone with a particular disability (mobility, sensory or cognitive) moves through a facility. This concept is established through the definition of an accessible route, either exterior or interior, and the elements along that route or at the destination that might be a barrier to an individual with that particular disability.

Scoping Provisions

The scoping provisions of the guidelines (ADAAG) apply to all areas of new construction with first occupancy after January 26, 1993 and altered portions of existing buildings completed after January 26, 1992. Exceptions are limited to those areas which can meet the requirements of ADA as "structurally impracticable" to build (a rare exception dealing mainly with site issues) and the following service areas: elevator pits, elevator penthouses, piping and equipment catwalks, lookout galleries or non-occupiable spaces accessed only by ladders, catwalks, crawl spaces, very narrow passageways, a freight (non-passenger) elevator, and frequented for repair purposes by service personnel.

Special provisions are provided for the following occupancies: restaurants/cafeterias, medical care facilities; business/mercantile, libraries, and accessible transient lodging. Special occupancy provisions can be applied even if that area only makes up a portion of the total facility although they apply only to that portion.

Areas defined as workstations for employees (who may be disabled) must be designed to allow accessible approach, entry and exit. All racks and shelves are not required to be accessible inside each workstation.

The requirements of ADAAG are to be applied to "temporary structures" also, including (but not limited to); reviewing stands, bleachers, temporary classrooms, bank facilities or health screening facilities, exhibit areas and temporary pedestrian passageway around construction sites. Elements including sites, structures, and equipment "directly associated with the actual process of construction" are exempt.

At least one accessible route shall be provided to connect the parking, bus stops, streets and sidewalks to the accessible buildings and elements of the site. Parking and signage requirements are also quantified in the scoping portion of the guidelines.

Scoping provisions are also provided to designate requirements for elements within newly constructed, altered and historic facilities along with the requirements associated with additions to existing facilities.

As mentioned above, we are not intending to substitute this workbook for the ADA Accessibility Guidelines, only to present some of the requirement highlights and touch on some of the key elements outlined therein.

For your convenience and so you can go right to the source, we have included in the workbook a complete copy of the ADA Accessibility Guidelines as printed in the Federal Register on July 26, 1991. All references to illustrations or figures are to those illustrations found in the ADA (ADAAG) Accessibility Guidelines.

Exterior Accessible Route

In this presentation we will address exterior accessible route elements which include parking issues, ramps, curb ramps, walks, gratings, changes in level, doormats and protruding hazards.

The first overall concept that we need to deal with, as we review all of these accessibility concerns, is the issue of **"accessible route"**. The ADA Accessibility Guidelines (ADAAG) defines it as follows:

> Accessible Route—A continuous unobstructed path connecting all accessible elements and spaces of a building or facility. Interior accessible routes may include corridors, floors, ramps, elevators, lifts and clear floor space at fixtures. Exterior accessible routes may include parking access aisles, curb ramps, crosswalks at vehicular ways, walks, ramps, and lifts.

The route must begin at the street and include any public transportation stops incorporating curb cuts and other elements that allow access to public transportation and also proceed past accessible or handicap parking and eventually lead to the building and its accessible entrance. The maximum slope for any portion of this path or **"accessible route"** is 1:20. If, at any point along the "accessible route", the slope is greater than 1:20, an engineered ramp must be incorporated meeting the handicap ramp requirements, so as to provide those with disabilities a suitable path to the building.

The ADAAG requires that there be, for new construction, at least one accessible route within the "boundary of the site" and that it should provide access from public transportation stops, accessible parking and accessible passenger loading zones, as well as public streets or sidewalks near the building, all the way up to the building and the building's accessible entrance.

Parking Issues

Handicapped parking spaces are required for those individuals that are "mobility impaired" or may have a serious health impairment that would limit the distance that they can comfortably walk from the car to the building. The ADAAG incorporates within their standards, **"scoping provisions"** that help to dictate the number of parking spaces required for a particular facility. Be sure to check the ADAAG and your local zoning ordinance, as it may require more or less accessible parking under certain circumstances. You are required to incorporate the most stringent requirement into your design.

The handicap spaces should be close to the accessible entrance (200 feet maximum preferred) and if at all possible, allow those with disabilities to access the building without crossing lanes of traffic, nor passing behind other parked cars. Many times, children and those in wheelchairs have a lower visible profile and are not seen passing behind parked cars, and can run the risk of having someone back out of a space and run over them.

The size of the space, in the ADAAG, is required to be at least 8'-0" wide with a 5'-0" wide (or 8' wide for van accessible space) adjacent aisle for access to and from the side of a vehicle (See Figure 9). You can gang two parking spaces along a single adjacent aisle if you prefer. The length of the parking space is usually determined by local zoning ordinance.

The ADA Guidelines also require a "van accessible" space for each 8 accessible spaces and, when van parking is provided for disabled people, a minimum of 98" vertical clearance along the route to a level handicapped parking space. This allows those disabled individuals who have specially equipped vans to maneuver into the handicapped parking space. This particular concern is an important issue when addressing handicap parking space needs at parking decks or structures, which usually have a height limitation much less than that required by the guidelines.

It is also required that the parking space and its adjacent aisle be relatively level, that is, have less than a 1:50 slope.

Ramps

Although we are addressing ramps under the major issues of site concerns, the requirements are the same for any ramp along an accessible route, be it inside a building, or outside a building. It should be noted that ramps are not the best way for individuals with disabilities to get around. It is far better if the site grading is designed for accessibility and ramps are not required.

It is required that along the accessible route, no changes in levels over 1/2" (i.e., steps or stairways) should be incorporated without the inclusion of a ramp (or elevator or lift). The maximum slope for a **ramp** in new construction is 1:12 but the ADAAG requires the "least possible slope" be used on any ramp as not all disabled individuals can easily negotiate a ramp with a slope of 1:12. It is required that **landings** be incorporated in ramps so that the maximum vertical rise between a landing or resting space is no greater than 30 inches. The minimum **width** of the ramp is 36 inches. Consideration should be given to those installations that provide sufficient space for a person in a wheelchair and a walking person to pass each other. It is preferred that ramp widths be increased accordingly.

Each **landing** is required to be a minimum of 5'-0" in length and as wide as the ramp (minimum). If it occurs at a change in direction, it can be no less than 5'-0" in width and 5'-0" in length. The landings that occur at entrances are very important as they must allow extra space so people using mobility aids can position themselves outside the door swing and have sufficient space to open the door.

If the rise of the ramp is greater than six inches or if the ramp's length is greater than six feet, then the ramp should be equipped with **handrails** on both sides (not required in sloping assembly spaces—only one side). The handrails should be continuous along the inside edge of the ramp and continue along the inside corner as levels change. Each handrail should extend at least 12 inches past the sloping segment at the top and bottom of the ramp. The clear space between the inside edge of the rail and the wall should be no greater nor less than 1-1/2 inches. The top of the rail should be located between 34 and 38 inches above the level of the ramp and the ends of the rail should be rounded or returned smoothly. **Curbs** should be incorporated to prevent wheelchairs from going outside the ramped area if the ramp is not enclosed in walls or does not have a guardrail or extended platform area to each side. (See Figure 17).

The ramp should have a cross slope of less than 1:50 and should also be designed to minimize ponding and address ice concerns in wintery weather. Ramps and curb ramps that are to be constructed in **existing buildings** or on existing sites may have slopes and rises slightly steeper than those required above. If the maximum rise of the ramp is three inches or less, the ramp can have a slope between 1:10 and 1:8. If the maximum rise is between three and six inches, the ramp can have a slope between 1:12 and 1:10. Note that no ramp is allowed to have a slope steeper than 1:8. These steeper ramp allowances are only applicable if space limitations prohibit the use of a ramp with a slope of 1:12 or less.

Curb Ramps

The street curb is probably the first architectural barrier that a disabled person will come to at your facility and the initial determining factor as to whether they will be able to access your facility. Also a major determining factor as to whether those with disabilities will be able to enter your facility or not is if they can get from the level of the street or drive to the level of the sidewalk. This is accommodated by the inclusion of **"curb ramps"**.

There are three typical and acceptable curb ramp designs. The first two designs (flared and returned) incorporate ramps that are outside the boundary of the street or parking area and are shown in **Figure 12.**

ADA Facilities Compliance™
7-92

The third type of curb ramp is a built-up ramp that is within the parking or street area and has flared sides as shown in **Figure 13.** The main ramped portion of the curb ramp is limited to a maximum slope of 1:12 or 1 inch rise in 12 inches of run. The flared sides of appropriate curb ramps, as in **Figure 12(a)** and **Figure 13** have a maximum slope of 1:10. Of the three curb ramp options presented here, the preferred design is that of the returned curb as shown in **Figure 12(b)** and should have planting and other non-walking surfaces alongside the curb return as shown in the drawing.

It is interesting to note, the advantages found by incorporating curb ramps for those who are in wheelchairs turn into disadvantages for the visually impaired who use canes to signal changes in levels and to determine where the street is. This is one of the few instances where cross disabilities conflict in their benefits. Because of the concern for the visually impaired, the ADA Guidelines (ADAAG) requires **detectable warnings** to designate where these curb ramps are located along the **"accessible route".** Truncated domes make up the detectable warning and should be incorporated into the full depth and width of the curb ramp.

Walks

Walks should be between four and five feet wide, but are actually required to be no less than three feet wide. They should be constructed of a smooth hard material and their surface should be **slip resistant.** The accessible route should not include sidewalks that are loose gravel, sand, pine bark or any other material that might catch a wheelchair wheel or might not support the concentrated load of crutches as they are utilized in the moving of a disabled person along the path. Again, the walks should not have a slope greater than 1:20 unless ramp provisions are incorporated.

Efforts should be made in the design of walks to prevent wheelchair wheels from rolling off the walk and dropping to the level of grade. In this case many wheelchairs will overturn and users are at risk of injury.

Building Approach

Another major issue in dealing with the accessibility needs of a particular facility is the **building approach.**

The most accessible entrance is that entrance which has the least vertical rise required from the parking area to the floor of the facility. Typically, this is the **grade level entrance.** ADAAG requires, under their minimum requirements, that "accessible entrances" when all entrances are not accessible, shall be identified by the **international symbol for accessibility.** (See Figure 43). For buildings in which all entrances are not accessible, inaccessible entrances must have directional signage indicating the route to the nearest accessible entrance.

In addition to these designated accessible entrances, parking spaces and loading zones reserved for those with disabilities and accessible toilet facilities are required to be identified by the use of the international symbol for accessibility.

Another main feature of any accessible entrance is its relative proximity to the **elevator lobby** (if an elevator is provided) or its proximity to a central circulation space from which interior accessible paths of travel might begin. Accessible entrances may or may not need to be ramped, but if a ramp is needed, yet impossible to construct due to, for example, site conditions, then a wheelchair lift is an acceptable alternative to a ramp to make an entrance accessible.

Gratings

Gratings, which are typically used in the ventilation of basement areas, in drainage systems, or as walk- off mats, must have slots that are 1/2" wide or less and are positioned perpendicular to the direction of the travel. This, again, is a requirement to allow ease of rolling for wheelchairs and to lessen the likelihood that a crutch tip or high heel shoe might be trapped inside the grating (See **Figure 8h).**

Changes In Level

The ADA Guidelines state that changes in level along an accessible route shall be limited to 1/2" and the edges should be beveled if the level change is between 1/4" and 1/2" and need not be beveled if the level changes is a maximum of 1/4" difference. If there is more than 1/2" level change, then a curb ramp, ramp, elevator, or platform lift must be provided.

A reason behind the concern for even such small level changes is that the front wheels of wheelchairs are very small in diameter and do not take level changes very well. A second reason is that people may, in fact, trip on the forward edge of a level change and hurt themselves. Thirdly, the blind person is more apt to be tripped if unexpected level changes are incorporated along the accessible path.

Doormats

Doormats are common in most commercial facilities and facilities of public accommodation. The hazards associated with doormats include the binding of the front wheels of a wheelchair if the mat is not firmly attached to the floor or the tripping of an individual if the mat bunches under a shuffling foot motion. The mats are required under this standard to be slip-resistant and should not be a carpet with a total pile thickness greater than 1/2".

Protruding Hazards

The people most likely to be hampered by protruding hazards or obstructions are the visually impaired. Objects projecting from the walls like public telephones or building directories, pose threats to those walking along the accessible route unaware of their projection. (See **Figure 8).** Another concern for visually impaired people is that of objects hanging from the ceiling. ADAAG requires that head room in halls, walkways, corridors be a minimum of 80 inches and if the head room along the accessible route is reduced to less than that, a barrier to warn the blind or visually impaired must be provided.

Other hazards might include: polished marble floors along the accessible route, that when wet can become slippery and inaccessible to one who is using crutches to move around; or, open tread stairs which are inaccessible and a tripping hazard to those who are mobility disabled and wear leg braces. To give you a better understanding of how a visually impaired person navigates through the environment using a cane, we have included **Figure A4,** which shows the typical cane sweeping patterns.

Interior Accessible Route

Accessibility requirements of the law can be, in some cases, as varied as the different types of businesses there are in our country. In the section that follows, we will address those concerns typically found in most facilities, such as doors, water fountains, bathroom facilities, telephones, elevators, corridors, to name a few.

Corridor Widths

At this point in our review of the needs of people with disabilities, we will focus on the issues of wheelchair maneuverability and space requirements even though the definition of a disability is much broader than just people who use wheelchairs. Note in **Figure 1** that the minimum clear width for a single wheelchair at a given point is 32", and along the corridor is 36" wide. As **Figure 2** shows, the minimum clear width for the passage of two wheelchairs is 60".

Figure 3 incorporates diagrams which explain how wheelchairs can be maneuvered to make 180 degree turns. This is very important and you will note that most handicap codes require the **five foot minimum turning diameter** in those rooms, such as restrooms, that typically have tight maneuvering spaces for those in wheelchairs. This radius is usually shown on the plans for the room as a dash or drawn circle.

As we saw previously in the illustration of the condition allowing the passage of two wheelchairs, the following illustration (**Figure A-1**) shows the minimum passage width for a wheelchair and one walking person.

In those instances where more than the minimum five foot space is provided, **Figure A-2** illustrates that space needed for a smooth 180 degree turn of a wheelchair. For those of you who are not familiar with the general design and configuration of a typical adult size wheelchair, **Figure A-3** illustrates standard dimensions that can be utilized to understand the space requirements for those who travel by wheelchair.

Figure 7 demonstrates the **minimum corridor requirements** at turns and also illustrates the issue of level changes which was mentioned previously.

Although the diagrams referred to previously illustrate typical elements of adult size wheelchairs, keep in mind that other standard types of wheelchairs are in use such as **electrically powered wheelchairs,** electrically powered scooters, and those wheelchairs modified for individuals who are smaller, larger or obese. In these cases, the dimensions shown in our typical illustrations above would need to be changed slightly to accommodate the actual conditions of those particular wheelchairs. Also note that even though corridors and passages are designed for the clearances of wheelchairs, consideration should be made also for use of **"walkers"** by ambulatory individuals with mobility impairment.

Doors

All doors on the accessible route are required to allow a minimum 32" **clear passage width. (See Figure 24).** The clear width of existing doors is of critical importance as this is a true architectural barrier if the clear width does not allow passage for people who use wheelchairs.

The **maneuvering clearances at doors** that do not have automatic or power assisted openers is critical and shall be as per **Figure 25.** The essence of the requirement is to allow the person in a wheelchair to maneuver his or her chair adjacent to the door handle and back-up with one hand while the other hand holds the door open. Then he or she may wheel in with one hand as the door is being restrained. This element of accessible design is very critical for those in wheelchairs and makes access to rooms without the required minimum maneuvering clearance very, very difficult.

Take special note that the doors that are located in alcoves must comply with the maneuvering clearances set forth for front approach doors. The size of the alcove, when designing new construction, must include the consideration for adjacent space next to the door handle.

Vestibules

With the advent of the energy crisis in the seventies, the installation of vestibules on many facilities became popular. One draw back of the use of **vestibules** is the potential for inaccessibility by those who use wheelchairs. The ADA guidelines have strict regulations that should be incorporated in your new construction and alteration projects. It might also be wise to consider the removal of or renovation of existing **vestibules** that do not comply with this regulation as it might be seen as an **architectural barrier** (as described under Section 302 of ADA) and potentially considered discriminatory against a disabled individual if not removed. Remember that the removal of architectural barriers must be "readily achievable". The major consideration in vestibules is the maneuvering clearance within the vestibule and the swing of the doors. The minimum maneuvering clearance for **doors in series** (as in a vestibule) is given in Figure 26 below.

Note that it is also an egress safety concern, in most instances, if the vestibule doors do not open in the direction of exiting traffic. Another alternative to the potential removal of an inaccessible entrance vestibule is the addition of an accessible entrance adjacent to the inaccessible vestibule entrance. This is commonly done at entrances that utilize **revolving doors.**

Please note that both doors of a vestibule should never open into the vestibule as this could potentially trap a person using a wheelchair in the vestibule. The same consideration should be made for those vestibules that require a 90 degree turn to enter or through which you might exit. Care must be taken that the required maneuvering room is provided.

Thresholds

The ADAAG mandates that no **door threshold** shall be over 1/2" high in its profile, except for those of sliding exterior doors which have a height limitation of 3/4". Note that if the threshold is over 1/4" high, a beveled profile must be provided for wheelchairs to bump over and to lessen the risk of tripping.

Door Hardware

The **door hardware** on new construction and alterations is extremely important to those with disabilities as many do not have the dexterity to turn a door knob. For this reason, accessible doors should have hardware that is shaped so that it is easy to grasp with one hand and does not require tight grasping or pinching or twisting of the wrist to operate. Lever-operated mechanisms, push type mechanisms and U-shaped handles are the acceptable designs of the ADAAG. Note also that for sliding doors, the operating hardware should still be exposed when the door is fully open and recall that the minimum clear opening width must be no less than 32".

Another potential architectural barrier to a person with disabilities is the **door closer,** which is utilized to automatically close the door after one has passed through it. It is important that the pressure setting on the closer is not beyond that which has been established as the maximum that a disabled person can operate. A suggested maximum for exterior hinged doors is 8-1/2 pounds opening force and is derived from the ANSI A117.1 Code. (This element is currently "reserved" in the ADAAG). Care should be taken to coordinate this requirement with closer force settings required for "fire doors" and exterior doors subject to winds or high building pressures. Automatic openers or power assisted closers might be required. Interior hinged and sliding doors are not allowed to require more than five pounds of pressure to open the door. In most cases, in existing facilities a fish scale can be used as a very easy test to ascertain the force required to open the door and the closer can be adjusted to comply with the regulations.

It is noted in the ADAAG that the utilization of **kick plates** on doors with closers can dramatically reduce the required maintenance of that door by allowing it to withstand bumps from the toe plates of wheelchairs. The same is true when considering the height of the sill in "storefront" windows that might otherwise go to the floor. Kick plates should be no less than 8" high (16" high is preferred) and no less than 2" less than the overall width of the door and placed on the push side of the door.

Stairs/Steps

In new construction, under the scoping provisions of the ADA Accessibility Guidelines (ADAAG) stairs connecting levels that are not connected by an elevator shall comply with the following requirements. Steps shall have uniform riser heights and uniform tread widths with the stair treads being not less than 11" deep measured from riser to riser. Open risers are not permitted in new construction where levels are not connected by an elevator. The front edge or nosing of each step cannot be squared off in its design nor can the undersides of the nosing be abrupt. The radius of the curvature at the leading edge of the tread cannot be greater than 1/2". The vertical part of the step, or riser, shall be either slopped or the underside of the nosing shall have an angle not less than 60 degrees from the horizontal. This allows for individuals that wear leg braces and have fixed foot positions to ride the riser up and over the steps. If a squared off nosing were in place then it is highly probable that the individual's toe would get caught under the nosing and they would trip. It is important to note that the maximum extension of the angled or rounded nosing can be no more than 1 1/2". For outdoor stairs, the steps and approaches shall be designed so that no water accumulates on the walking surfaces. This will lessen the chance of slipping on either wet surfaces or ice that might build up in cold conditions.

Handrails are required on both sides of all stairs per ADAAG requirement. The inside handrail must be continuous with the switchback on dog-leg stairs. If either of the handrails are not continuous, they shall extend at least 12" beyond the top of the riser and at least 12" plus the width of one tread beyond the bottom riser. At the top, the extension shall be parallel with the floor or ground surface and at the bottom the handrail shall continue to slope for a distance the width of one tread from the bottom riser with the reminder of the extension horizontal. Handrails shall be constructed so that they are not interrupted by newel posts or other construction elements or obstructions and shall have a clear space of 1 1/2" between the handrail and the wall.

Mounting heights for handrail gripping surfaces shall be between 34" and 38" above the stair nosing. The ends of the handrail shall be either rounded or returned smoothly to the floor wall on posts. Handrails shall not be loose or able to rotate within their fittings.

Railings

The issue of **railings** is of considerable import, as many children each year die or are injured by squeezing through and falling. This issue is one that must be considered if the installation of a ramp is required and your local building code requires that a **"guard rail"** be provided. Typically guard rails are required in those situations where the difference in levels is more than 30". The height of the rail is typically 42" and most codes require that the space between the top of the railing and the floor be designed so that a 6" sphere may not pass through. Note that current proposals are suggesting that this dimension should be reduced to 4". Also required, is the installation of an intermediate **hand rail** for stabilizing oneself if the guard rail is 42" off the floor. This "hand rail" must be provided between 34" and 38" off the floor, typically. Hand rail and guard rail requirements can often be confusing and usually need special attention from your design professional to insure proper placement.

Controls and Operating Mechanisms

The ADAAG requires floor space that allows for a forward or a parallel approach by a person using a wheelchair so that those individuals can **operate controls** or utilize dispensers and other operable equipment. The height of the operable part of all controls, dispensers, receptacles, and other **operable equipment** shall not be higher than 48" if the approach is from the front and 54" if the approach is from the side. Operating controls shall require a force of five pounds or less and should not require tight grasping, pinching or twisting of the wrist as these feats of dexterity, for some disabled individuals, would not allow them access to the controls.

It is important to note that all **electrical** and **telephone** outlets on the walls shall be mounted no less than 15" above the floor to allow those in wheelchairs access to them. With regard to control reach limitations, see the accompanying drawing designated **Figure A-8.**

Elevators

As we saw in Section 303 of the law, elevators are required in all facilities except those with less than three stories or those that have exceptionally small floor areas. **Elevators,** again, are elements that can be exceedingly frustrating to disabled people, more particularly, those who are visually impaired and those who use wheelchairs.

When considering accessible aspects of required elevators, you must address the issue that they be located on an **accessible route** through the building. They need also include an **auto leveling device** that brings the elevator within 1/2" of the floor so that the risk of tripping is limited. With regard to car controls, **Figure 23** designates their proper location, given the different types of elevator configurations. Interior **cab controls** should be located on the wall no higher than 48" except in instances where side approach is possible, in which case the maximum mounting height may be increased to 54" off the floor. Note the panel detail of **Figure 23** in the location of emergency alarm and stop controls.

Figure 20 defines the location of elements, such as floor identification plaques on the side of the elevator door jambs, hall lantern signals, elevator call buttons, and door protective and reopening devices (infrared beams).

The size of the elevator cars is extremely important to those who use wheelchairs, as without enough maneuvering room, the elevator is practically inaccessible. The **minimum dimensions for elevator cars** is designated in **Figure 22.**

In each elevator car, a visual car position indicator is required above the car control panel or over the door to show the position of the elevator in the hoistway. As the car passes or stops at each floor, corresponding numbers should be illuminated in an attempt to assist people with hearing impairments to ascertain at which floor they are arriving, and an **audible signal** should sound to help visually impaired persons designate at which level they are arriving.

Flooring

The ADAAG states that those "ambulant and semi- ambulant" that have difficulty maintaining their balance and those with "restricted gaits" are particularly sensitive to **tripping** and **slipping hazards.** For these people, it is critical that stable and regular ground or floor surface be provided particularly on stairs. Wheelchairs can be more easily moved along hard, stable and regular surfaces. Soft or loose surfaces such as shag carpet, loose sand and wet clay, grass, and irregular surfaces such as cobblestones or brick paving can "significantly impede" wheelchair movement.

The **slipping resistance** of a particular flooring surface is based upon the frictional force necessary to keep a shoe heel or crutch tip from slipping on that surface. The worst case is found on **wet** or **icy surfaces.** It was also noted that those cross-slopes that are not within the required minimums on walkways, ramps and floor surfaces cause considerable difficulty in moving a wheelchair in a straight line. A particular concern to those in wheelchairs is the issue of **heavily padded carpet,** as this condition can impede the movement of the wheelchair by binding its front wheels. The binding is a result of the carpet and the padding moving at different rates and a hump or warp creating an essentially immovable barrier.

Although the standards do not say that thick, padded carpet cannot be utilized, they do require that it is not utilized along the accessible route or path of travel to the primary functions of the building in areas where carpet is used along the accessible route. The elimination of the pad and gluing down the carpet will significantly decrease the likelihood of warping or binding along the front wheels of the wheelchair.

Toilet Rooms

The ADAAG requires that all public and common (employee) use toilets have at least one standard (and one 3' wide for 6 total stalls in a toilet room) stall for each sex, per floor, accessible and usable by disabled people and that all other toilet rooms be "adaptable". It would be wise to also check any local ordinances that might require more than one stall per floor in your particular location. If existing facilities do not have **accessible toilet stalls,** then a possible solution would be to provide one unisex handicap toilet. Another possible solution would be to remove an adjacent water closet unit and make what was two stalls into one accessible stall. This last option is predicated on the notion that more than one stall is provided in each restroom facility, and secondly that plumbing regulations adopted by your particular municipality would allow the removal of one existing stall.

Toilet stall configurations allowed by the ADAAG are shown in **Figure 30.** Take special note that the **standard stall** designated with (a) and (a-1) are the mandatory configuration for toilet stalls in new construction. These are also configurations required in alteration projects if space is available to accommodate these designs. If space is not available to accommodate these designs, **alternate stall** designs are shown in this drawing and designated as alternate stalls (b).

Note also in Figure 30 that the depth of the stalls depend upon the type of water closet utilized in the stall. If a **wall mounted water closet** is utilized, a shorter stall depth is allowed and if a **floor mounted water closet** is utilized, a longer stall depth is required.

All accessible toilet stalls shall be provided with **grab bars** in the configuration shown in **Figure 29.** The ADAAG makes it clear that many disabled persons rely heavily upon the grab bars to maintain balance and prevent serious falls. This standard also requires a 1-1/2 inch clearance between the wall and the innermost edge of the grab bar. The grab bars should be of a thickness between 1-1/4 inch to 1-1/2 inch in diameter.

As for all accessible passages, the **toilet stall door** is required to have no less than 32 inches clear for wheelchair passage. The door should open in the direction as shown in Figure 30. For your understanding, we have included a diagram (**Figure A-6**) that demonstrates the two different transfer approaches from wheelchair to water closet. They include the diagonal approach designated as (a) and the side approach designated as (b).

The ADAAG states for new construction, if toilet facilities are provided, "then each public and common use toilet room shall comply" and be accessible. If "other toilet rooms" are provided, then they "shall be **adaptable**". The term "adaptable or adaptability" is defined as the "ability of certain building spaces and elements such as kitchen counters, sinks and grab bars to be added or altered so as to accommodate the needs of either disabled or non-disabled persons or to accommodate the needs of persons with different types or degrees of disabilities". The issue of "other toilet rooms" seems to apply to those toilet facilities used primarily by certain employees and therefore we should not assume that these **employee restrooms** are exempt from accessibility concerns.

Urinals

If urinals are provided, the regulations require that at least one urinal be provided that is handicap accessible. Handicap accessible urinals should have a rim height no greater than 17" off of the floor and should be configured with an elongated bowl. The regulations also require that clear floor space be provided around the urinal with a minimum 30" width and a minimum 48" depth.

Lavatories and Mirrors

Mirrors and lavatories are of particular concern to people who use wheelchairs, as is the accessibility of toilet room lavatories and the mirrors in toilet rooms. Frequently, poorly designed, inaccessible **lavatories** or **vanities** will force a disabled individual to postpone cleaning up after using the bathroom. This is exceptionally disappointing if the individual has had to empty a colostomy bag. Therefore, the ADAAG stipulates that the lavatories shall be mounted with a rim or counter surface no higher than 34" above the finish floor to allow access to the sink or lavatory and require that a minimum knee clearance of 29" be provided from the bottom of the apron or underside of the front edge of the lavatory. (See **Figure 31**).

The regulations also state that a clear floor space of at least 30" wide and 48" deep be provided around the individual accessible lavatory (see **Figure 32**).

Another particularly upsetting condition that is found frequently by those who use wheelchairs is the unprotected nature of **hot water pipes** and drain pipes underneath the lavatories. For those who have lost feeling in their lower limbs, contact with the hot water pipe or the drain (if hot water has been poured down it) can cause severe burns and go unnoticed. The remedy for this is in the guidelines, which require insulation to be wrapped around the hot water pipe and the drain pipe to eliminate the risk of burns, or the installation of a suitable accessible protective skirt or cover to enclose the pipe so that legs cannot come into contact with them.

The guidelines also require **faucet handles** to be of either the lever-type, push type or electronically controlled mechanisms. When self-closing valves are used, the faucet should remain open for at least ten seconds.

With regard to **mirrors,** the standards require that the bottom edge of the reflecting surface be no higher than 40" from the floor. If mirrors are to be used by both ambulatory people and wheelchair users, then they must be at least 74" high at their topmost edge. It is suggested a single, **full length mirror** be incorporated in the design of the toilet room facilities for use by both ambulatory and wheelchair users, and by children. If adjustable mirrors are installed that tilt to offer a better view for the disabled, then they should remain in the tilted mode as those in wheelchairs cannot typically reach the top of the mirror to activate the mechanism that tilts the mirrors.

Toilet Room Accessories

Our discussion on toilet room accessories should begin with toilet paper dispensers. They are required in the guidelines to be situated no lower than 19" above the floor and a maximum distance of 36" from the rear wall. Other toilet room accessories such as paper towel dispensers, toilet seat cover dispensers, sanitary napkin dispensers and disposal units, waste receptacles, air hand dryers, soap dispensers and vending machines must all have at least one unit within the 48"/54" reach limit of individuals using wheelchairs.

Alarms

Fire alarms and other **audible alarms** are required to limit their output not to exceed 120 decibels. **Visual alarms** shall flash at less than 5 hz. and be tied into the emergency power circuit. Fire alarms should also incorporate visual strobes to alert individuals who are deaf or hearing impaired.

Public Telephones

If **public telephones** are provided, then at least one per floor should be accessible to and usable by individuals with disabilities. This means that it should have a clear floor space as shown in Figure 44. The **cord** length on the telephone handset should be at least 29" and an adjustable **volume control** should be provided. Telephone books, if provided, should be located in a position that is within reach of those in wheelchairs. The controls on the telephone should be **push-button controls** where the service is available.

Although telecommunication concerns are under **Title IV** of the ADA and require further telephone accessibility, i.e., **"TDD"** (telecommunication devices for the deaf) the ADAAG requires TDD units in facilities providing 4 or more public telephones as well as in other special circumstances.

Work Surfaces

In general, work surfaces such as countertops, library tables, dining tables and the like will be accessible if their height ranges between 28" and 34" above the floor. It is required that 27" of **clear knee space** be allowed under the table, and this knee space shall be a minimum of 30" wide and 19" deep. An example of clearances for seating and tables is presented in **Figure 45**.

Also included for your convenience is a chart of heights associated with varying tasks and individual requirements. (See **Table A-1).** This chart reflects the different types of requirements as demanded by different types of work and work surfaces that are required for the performance of those tasks. ADAAG suggests that the principal of high work surface height for **light detailed work** (such as writing), and the low work surface for **heavy manual work** (such as rolling out dough), also applies for seating individuals who use a wheelchair However, the limiting condition for seated manual work is the clearance under the work surface.

Interior Finishes

We have already discussed concerns about certain flooring types, but we should address issues for **interior finish elements.** Specialists have stated that the use of darker or high contrast **baseboards** along corridors, and in some accessible rooms, is very beneficial to those who are visually impaired and who have a difficult time distinguishing between the wall plane and the floor plane. Researchers have also expressed concerns over the installation of certain wall coverings with dynamic, **contrasting**

geometric patterns, which when seen in a serial progression (like walking down a corridor), may trigger epileptic seizures in individuals with seizure disorders.

Also a potential trigger of epileptic seizures and a potential distraction to the mentally challenged is the use of certain **fluorescent light fixtures** whose bulbs are clearly visible. It seems that under certain circumstances, the frequency of the light produced in some fluorescent fixtures may also trigger seizures in this group of individuals. Keep in mind that these are not design mandates, but helpful considerations for those of you who may deal with these groups of the disabled.

Signage

The ADA guidelines require that all permanent room or space identification signs except those displaying temporary information on room or space signage (such as current occupants name) must meet the following requirements. The letters and numbers of the signs must have a width to height ratio between 3:5 and 1:1 and a stroke width to height ratio between 1:5 and 1:10. Characters and symbols must also contrast in their color or image with either light letters on dark background or dark letters on light background.

Letters and numbers on permanent room identification signs shall be raised 1/32" minimum, shall be sans serif, upper case characters and shall be accompanied by Grade 2 Braille. The minimum height for raised characters or symbols is 5/8" but no higher than 2". Pictographs (such as images of a woman or man on a restroom door) must also be accompanied by the equivalent verbal description directly below. Interior signs shall be located alongside the door on the latch side and shall be centered at a height of 60" above the floor.

Many more requirements are outlined in the ADAAG for signage including finish requirements and contrast requirements.

Water Fountains

If drinking fountains are provided, and they are almost always required under local or state ordinances, then half of those provided on each floor shall comply with the accessibility requirements outlined below. If only one **drinking fountain** is provided on any floor, it shall be accessible to people who use wheelchairs (see **Figure 27)** and shall have a higher unit for those who can't stoop over.

Accessible drinking fountains must be located on an **accessible route.** If they are located in an **alcove,** typically that alcove can be no more than 24 inches deep nor less than 30 inches wide. (See **Figure 27).**

As is evident in the ADAAG Drinking Fountain drawing, the spout height is to be no more than 36 inches above the floor and the unit must allow for the appropriate approach and maneuvering "clear floor space".

If you are in an existing facility with an inaccessible water cooler or drinking fountain, a possible solution to the "readily achievable removal of (that) architectural barrier" might be to install a **cup dispenser** with which a disabled person would then have access to that drinking fountain. Note also that hygiene concerns might also make this option attractive.

Special Occupancies

In this section of our discussion about facility accessibility, we will touch briefly upon some special building types. The ADA Accessibility Guidelines limit the coverage of **special occupancy concerns** to: restaurants/cafeterias; medical care facilities, (such as hospitals); business and mercantile spaces; libraries; and transient lodging facilities. It is expected that ATBCB is going to supplement their accessibility regulations with requirements for even more special occupancy types such as playgrounds, stadia, and amusement parks.

Restaurants/Cafeterias

Even if your business is not a restaurant, most major corporations have **cafeteria facilities** and the accessibility issues that will be presented below should be incorporated in those facilities. ADAAG requires that **five percent** of all the fixed tables in the dining area be accessible to and usable by individuals with a disability. (For more information on characteristics of accessible tables, see heading titled "Work Surfaces" presented previously.) Where practical, accessible tables should be distributed throughout the space or facility.

In cafeterias or restaurants that incorporate design elements such as **mezzanines** or raised platform areas, access to these areas is required.

In cafeteria settings the **food service lines** should be a minimum of 36" wide and preferably should be 42" wide where a stopped wheelchair could be passed by pedestrians. The tray line should be mounted no higher than 34" above the floor, and self service shelves for such things as napkins, forks, and trays should be provided within reach of those in wheelchairs. See **Figure 53** for a food service line illustration. Where **vending machines** and other dispensary elements are provided, they should be accessible to people with disabilities. For more information on this element, please see information presented previously on the accessibility of controls and operating mechanisms.

Medical Care Facilities

All healthcare facilities are required to have an accessible entrance that is protected by a **canopy** and allows for the covered unloading of disabled passengers. Long term care facilities such as **nursing homes** are required to have at least 50% of all patient toilets and bedrooms accessible. All common or public use spaces must also be accessible and all areas to which handicapped employees may need access are required to be accessible.

Outpatient facilities such as day clinics and med- surg clinics are not 24 hour care facilities and therefore not covered by this section, but it would be wise to have all patient toilets and exam rooms accessible. All common or public use spaces along with those utilized by disabled employees must be handicap accessible.

In **full service hospitals,** psychiatric and detox facilities, at least 10% of all patient toilets and patient rooms must be accessible. All common and public use spaces along with those spaces that could be utilized by a disabled employee must also be made accessible. All patient toilets in those facilities that treat conditions that affect mobility must be made accessible.

Patient room requirements under ADAAG include the requirement that a 360 degree or "T" shape turning space must be provided in the patient room that is required to be accessible and preferably located near the room entrance.

In **one bed patient rooms,** the accessible clearance area is 36" clear at the side and 36" clear at the foot of the bed.

In **two bed patient rooms,** the clearance is 36" between the side of the bed and the wall, 36" between beds, and 36" minimum (48" preferred) at the foot of the bed.

In **four bed patient rooms,** the clearances that are required include 36" between the side of the bed and the wall, 36" between the beds, and 36" clear at the foot of the bed.

All patient rooms shall be equipped with **accessible doorways.** This means that a minimum of 32" clear is required. (Most healthcare facilities are required, under codes other than UFAS, to have doors that are a minimum of 44" wide when they are placed in areas that are utilized by patients, in this case, maneuvering space per 4.13.6 is not required on the latch side of the door).

Patient toilet rooms that are required to be accessible shall have doors with a minimum 32" clear passage and shall not swing into the clear space required for any toilet room fixture. Water closet, bathing facilities, lavatories, mirrors, and other toilet accessories shall be accessible in toilet rooms provided in accessible patient rooms.

Business and Mercantile

For those of you who deal in **retail business,** the service counter at your facility should be provided with a portion (at least 36" wide) of the service counter that is at a height of not more than 36". For those counters that are over 36" high, an associated alternate accessible counter must be provided. A portion of all **check-out aisles,** when check-out aisles are provided, are required to be such that there is a minimum 36" width (32" minimum at any one point) and a counter height that does not exceed 38".

Security bollards, used to prevent theft of shopping carts, shall not prevent the passage of wheelchairs. An equally convenient alternate accessible entry may be provided to accommodate this requirement.

Libraries

Five percent or a minimum of one of each element of fixed seating must be accessible. Tables or study carrels shall be accessible as well as routes through these areas and other public areas.

At least one of the lanes at each **check-out area** shall be accessible and preferably all check-out lanes should be accessible. No security element (gates, bollards, or turnstiles) shall be installed without being accessible or without an alternative route provided for the disabled.

Card catalogs, when provided, shall allow for 36" clear (minimum) between the units and the units shall be no lower than 18" above the floor nor higher than 54" above the floor (see Figure 55). In libraries, shelf or stack heights are unrestricted but the passage and clear space between these elements is required to be no less than 36" with 42" preferred (see **Figures**

55 and 56). The Congressional Reports on ADA suggested that not all books be within the reach of those individuals who are disabled, but a system should be available, when requested, for the retrieval of books that are not within the reach of those who are disabled.

Transient Lodging

This section deals with facility requirements of the ADA Accessibility Guidelines for transient lodging facilities which include facilities or portions thereof used for sleeping accommodations when not classified as a medical care facility.

In hotels, motels, inns, boarding houses, dormitories, resorts and other similar places of transient lodging operated by a private entity, all public use and common uses (employee) areas must be designed to meet the accessibility requirements of Section 4 and Sections 9.2 and 9.3 of the ADA Accessibility Guidelines. A percentage (per Table at 9.1.2) of each class of sleeping rooms or suites are required to be designed and constructed to be accessible under the same sections. In addition to the requirements mentioned above, another portion of each class of sleeping rooms or suites, but never fewer than one, shall comply with the accessibility requirements in the ADAAG which relate to the special needs of people with hearing impairments. All rooms, including those designated to be accessible above, shall be on an accessible route and have doors or doorways designed so as to allow passage into and within all sleeping rooms. As you recall, the minimum clear door opening width is 32" and an established clear maneuvering space requirement is set forth in the door section of the ADAAG.

The special occupancy requirements do not apply to an establishment "located within a building that contains not more than 5 rooms for rent or hire and that is actually occupied by the proprietor of such establishment as the residence of such proprietor". This appears to be a rather limited exception.

In those rooms designated to be accessible by the requirements mentioned above, each shall have the space required for a wheelchair to make a 180 degree turn (60" diameter) or a T-shaped turning space. Within the unit, an accessible route with the appropriate forward and side reach limits and minimum 36" clear width, shall be provided so as to allow access to all accessible spaces and elements within the suite or sleeping room including telephones. All the doors and doorways within or leading into the suite or sleeping room must comply with the accessibility requirements for doors in Section 4.13 of the ADAAG. Storage areas, including cabinets, shelves, closets and drawers, within each accessible sleeping room or suite, must allow a clear floor space of at least 30" x 48" so that either forward or parallel approach by a person in a wheelchair can be made. The height of the storage spaces shall be within the reach ranges of 48" to 54" above the finished floor. Clothes rods shall be a maximum of 54" above the floor. Door and cabinet hardware shall be accessible (i.e., touch latches, U-shaped pulls, etc.). Electrical and telephone receptacles on the wall shall be mounted no less than 15" above the floor and all operational elements and controls, such as light switches, thermostats, and the like, must be within the reach ranges of 48" AFF (for a front approach) or 54" AFF (for a side approach).

The following areas, if provided within an accessible sleeping room or suite, shall themselves be designed for accessibility and be located on an accessible route:

A. the living area

B. the dining area

C. at least one sleeping area

D. patios, terraces, balconies, carports, garages, or parking spaces

E. at least one full bathroom (i.e., one with water closet, lavatory and a bathtub or shower)

F. if only half baths are provided, at least one half bath

G. carports, garages or parking spaces.

In addition, kitchens, kitchenettes, and/or wet bars, when provided within an accessible sleeping room or suite, must be designed for accessibility. Countertops and sinks shall have a maximum mounting height of 34" above the floor with a clear floor space (30" x 48") for a front or parallel approach to the cabinets, counters or sinks or appliances. Not less than 50% of the shelf space in cabinets and refrigerators/freezers shall be within the reach of a person in a wheelchair (i.e., 48" for front approach and 54" for side approach).

As mentioned above, no less than one of the non- accessible sleeping rooms and suites in the facility and all of the accessible sleeping room accommodations shall be provided with visual alarms and visual "notification devices". The visual "notification devices" shall be provided to alert those in the room who may have hearing impairments of incoming telephone calls or a door knock or bell. These visual "notification devices" shall not be connected to the visual alarm system. Those telephones which are permanently installed in each room or suite shall have volume controls.

In new homeless shelters, half-way houses, transient group homes, or other social service transient lodging facilities, all public use and common use areas are required to be designed and constructed to meet the accessibility requirements of Section 4 of the ADAAG. No less than one of each type of amenity such as clothes washers, dryers, and similar equipment installed for use by the occupants in each common area shall be accessible and it shall be located on an accessible route to or from any accessible unit or sleeping accommodation. Alterations to these homeless shelters and other similar facilities are not currently addressed in the ADAAG nor is the accessible sleeping accommodation portion of those facilities.

Building Codes and Other Concerns

As you begin to consider and address ADA compliance issues as they relate to your existing facilities and new construction projects, you must also be aware of the requirements of **other codes** and how they can affect the implementation of ADA compliance work. Issues that might conflict or have to be addressed as you set out to comply with these accessibility requirements of the ADA include structural concerns, egress or exiting requirements, electrical code requirements, plumbing code requirements, and any potential conflicts between these elements of building construction. Conflicts with other building codes and zoning ordinances may also complicate compliance.

Structural Concerns

These issues should not be of concern if you employ qualified design consultants to work with you on resolving ADA compliance issues. Potentially, though, structural issues in modifications to existing facilities might play a primary role. These issues may include the modification of a load bearing wall requiring additional support or lintel beams; or structural supports being required for the addition of an elevator or lift in an existing facility; or the issues of how you might tie in the concrete foundations of a new ramp to the existing foundation of your facility. Always consult an architect or structural engineer before attempting any structural modifications to the construction of any public accommodations or commercial facilities.

Exit Concerns

The ADA Accessibility Guidelines require that all accessible routes serving spaces or elements that are made accessible in new construction, also be able to be utilized as **means of exiting** in case of emergencies or connect to an acceptable **"area of rescue assistance"**. ADAAG also stresses that in areas where fire codes require more than one means of **"egress"** (exits), it is required that more than one accessible means of egress be provided for the disabled individual. It is also required that these exits be "readily accessible" from all rooms that could be used by the disabled. This issue is primarily a concern to those who are using wheelchairs, as they may become potential hostages in fire emergencies if they find themselves on floors that do not have grade level access. Imagine being on the twenty-eighth floor of a tall office building and being notified that because there is a fire on the floor below, the elevators are no longer in service and you are to find your own way out of this building. It would be a very frightening position in which to find yourself. This issue is addressed under the section on Areas of Rescue Assistance in the ADAAG and must be kept in mind when providing accessible spaces on floors above the grade level.

The guidelines require an area of rescue assistance to be one of seven options outlined in section 4.3.11. A two-way audio and visual system must be provided that connects each area of refuge to a central emergency management control point. The space shall be designed to accommodate two wheelchair spaces each 30" x 48". Doors must open in the direction of exit travel and the area shall have a one-hour minimum fire-resistive separation. A sign identifying and directing people to the area of refuge shall be installed and shall incorporate the "international symbol of accessibility".

Electrical Concerns

Before you modify any existing facility or construct any new facility, it is imperative that you consult an architect or an electrical engineer. He or she is qualified in determining the **electrical code requirements** for your facility and how those code requirements might relate to the proposed modifications, if you are changing your facility.

Be especially mindful of the **removal of walls** that may be hiding one or more electrical conduits. It is not that this situation cannot be dealt with, it is only that you must consider the cost and code ramifications of relocating existing electrical elements. Of special concern when dealing with this type relocation, is whether you run into an existing electrical panel in the wall that you might consider modifying to provide greater accessibility.

Plumbing Concerns

The same issues that are involved in the electrical concerns paragraph above are also involved when dealing with existing and future plumbing elements. Be especially mindful of **plumbing codes** when you are considering the modification of an existing restroom. You may not be allowed by the plumbing codes to remove one of your water closets in order to enlarge an adjacent one to comply with accessibility requirements.

Zoning Regulations

Your municipal zoning regulations will probably come into play as you begin to survey facilities for the required number of **handicapped parking spaces.** It is imperative that you not only utilize the federal standards to ascertain the proper number of handicapped parking spaces, but you must also review your local zoning ordinance or zoning code to ensure that your local municipality does not require more than that required by the federal standards. We will discuss in the next paragraph what to do when the requirements for compliance with ADA seem to conflict with those building, electrical, plumbing, or zoning codes.

Code Conflicts

As we mentioned above, it is imperative that you do not solely rely on the ADA final Guidelines, as they do not cover issues of plumbing, electrical, exiting, zoning, and other building related issues. It is also probable that your local municipality has adopted local regulations which their building inspector is authorized to enforce.

In brief, non-compliance to code requirements that are enforced by your local building official might result in that official **stopping work** on your project or electing not to issue your **"Certificate of Occupancy".** Issues relative to ADA compliance will typically be enforced through **civil suit** or through an **investigation** by the United States Attorney General. It is also very important to note that under Section 501 of ADA, you are required to comply with the more stringent state or local ordinance if it provides equal protection for the rights of those with disabilities. An example of a more stringent consideration might be the requirement for "detectable warnings" for the blind that is required under ANSI A117.1 which has been adopted by many municipalities but is **"reserved",** or not applicable, under parts of the current ADAAG.

*   *   *

Table 1
Graphic Conventions

Convention	Description
36 / 915	Typical dimension line showing U.S. customary units (in inches) above the line and SI units (in millimeters) below
9 / 230	Dimensions for short distances indicated on extended line
9 / 230 36 / 915	Dimension line showing alternate dimensions required
⇩	Direction of approach
max	Maximum
min	Minimum
••••••••••	Boundary of clear floor area
₵	Centerline

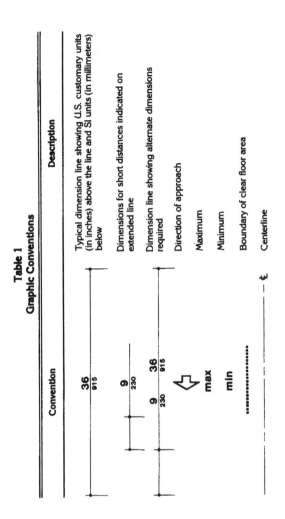

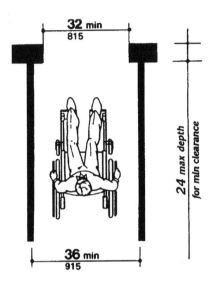

Fig. 1
Minimum Clear Width
for Single Wheelchair

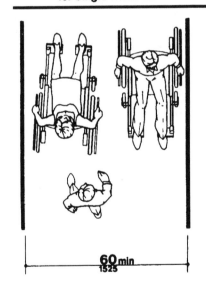

Fig. 2
Minimum Clear Width
for Two Wheelchairs

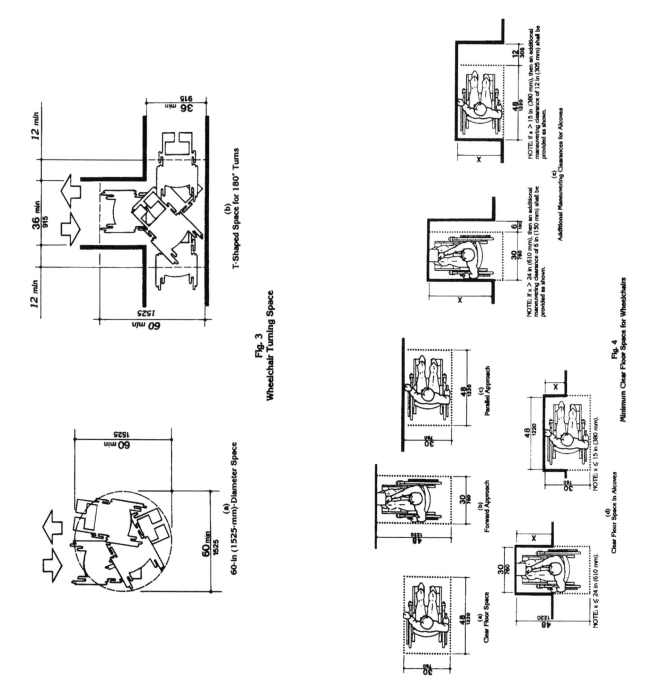

Fig. 3
Wheelchair Turning Space

Fig. 4
Minimum Clear Floor Space for Wheelchairs

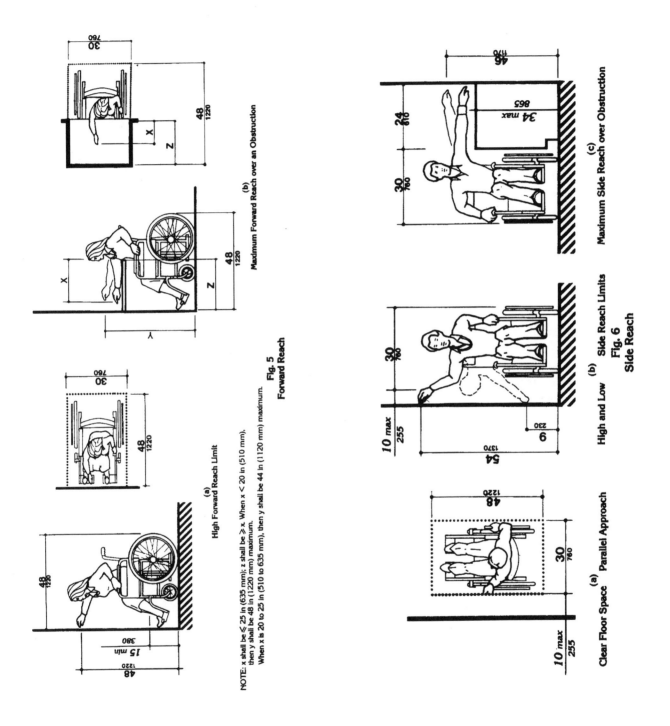

(a)
High Forward Reach Limit

(b)
Maximum Forward Reach over an Obstruction

NOTE: x shall be ≤ 25 in (635 mm); z shall be ≥ x. When x < 20 in (510 mm),
then y shall be 48 in (1220 mm) maximum.
When x is 20 to 25 in (510 to 635 mm), then y shall be 44 in (1120 mm) maximum.

Fig. 5
Forward Reach

(a) Clear Floor Space   Parallel Approach

(b) High and Low   Side Reach Limits

(c) Maximum Side Reach over Obstruction

Fig. 6
Side Reach

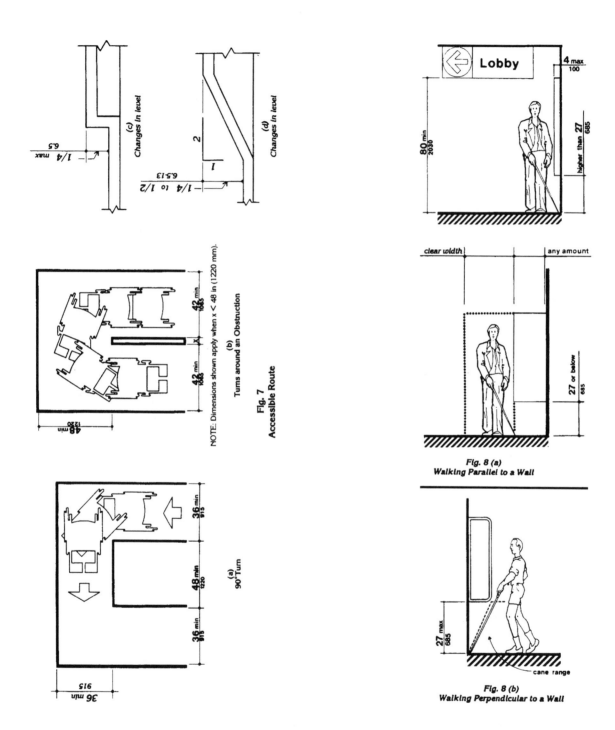

(c)
Changes in level

6.5

1/4 max

(d)
Changes in level

6.5-13

1/4 to 1/2

2

1

42 min
1065

42 min
1065

x

48 min
1220

(b)
Turns around an Obstruction

NOTE: Dimensions shown apply when x < 48 in (1220 mm).

Fig. 7
Accessible Route

36 min
915

48 min
1220

36 min
915

36 min
915

(a)
90° Turn

Lobby

4 max
100

80 min
2030

higher than 27
685

clear width

any amount

27 or below
685

Fig. 8 (a)
Walking Parallel to a Wall

27 max
685

cane range

Fig. 8 (b)
Walking Perpendicular to a Wall

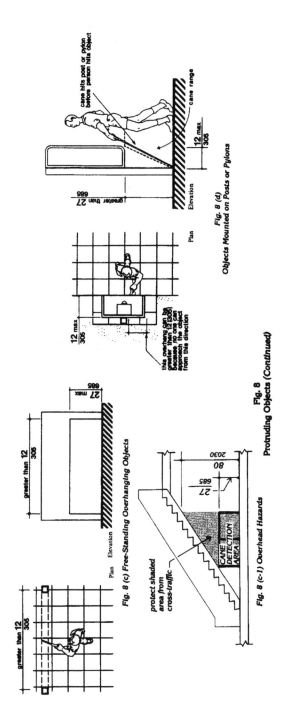

greater than 12
305

27 max
685

Plan   Elevation

Fig. 8 (c) Free-Standing Overhanging Objects

protect shaded
area from
cross-traffic

CANE
DETECTION
AREA

27
685

80
2030

Fig. 8 (c-1) Overhead Hazards

greater than 12
305

cane hits post or pylon
before person hits object

cane range

12 max
305

greater than 27
685

Elevation

Plan

12 max
305

this overhang can be
greater than 12 (305)
because no one can
approach the object
from this direction

*Fig. 8 (d)
Objects Mounted on Posts or Pylons*

**Fig. 8
Protruding Objects (Continued)**

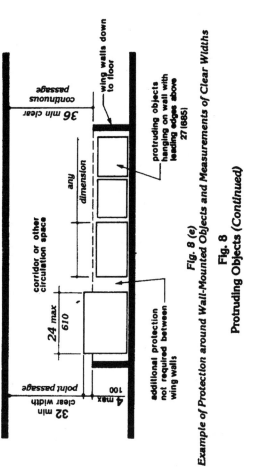

wing walls down
to floor

continuous
passage

36 min clear

protruding objects
hanging on wall with
leading edges above
27 (685)

any
dimension

corridor or other
circulation space

24 max
610

point passage

32 min
clear width

4 max
100

additional protection
not required between
wing walls

*Fig. 8 (e)
Example of Protection around Wall-Mounted Objects and Measurements of Clear Widths*

**Fig. 8
Protruding Objects (Continued)**

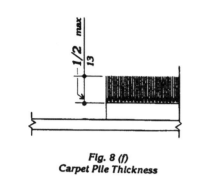

Fig. 8 (f)
Carpet Pile Thickness

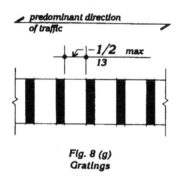

Fig. 8 (g)
Gratings

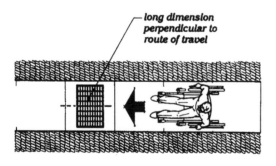

Fig. 8 (h)
Grating Orientation

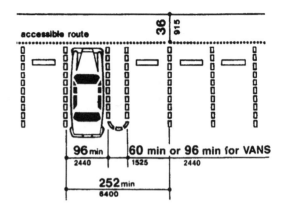

Fig. 9
Dimensions of Parking Spaces

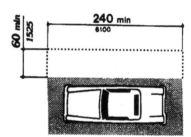

Fig. 10
Access Aisle at Passenger Loading Zones

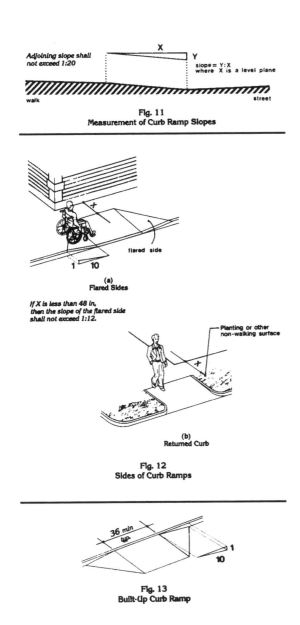

Fig. 11
Measurement of Curb Ramp Slopes

(a)
Flared Sides

If X is less than 48 in,
then the slope of the flared side
shall not exceed 1:12.

(b)
Returned Curb

Fig. 12
Sides of Curb Ramps

Fig. 13
Built-Up Curb Ramp

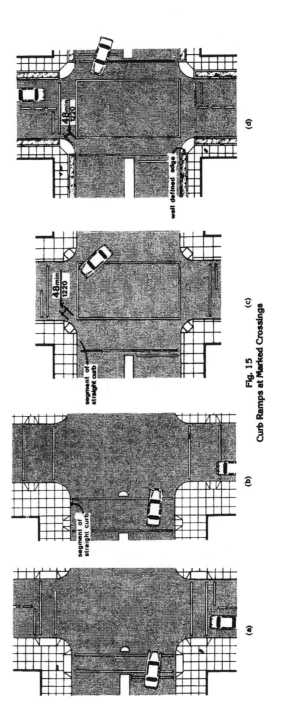

Fig. 15
Curb Ramps at Marked Crossings

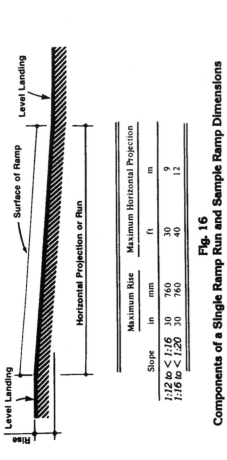

Slope	Maximum Rise		Maximum Horizontal Projection	
	in	mm	ft	m
1:12 to < 1:16	30	760	30	9
1:16 to < 1:20	30	760	40	12

Fig. 16
Components of a Single Ramp Run and Sample Ramp Dimensions

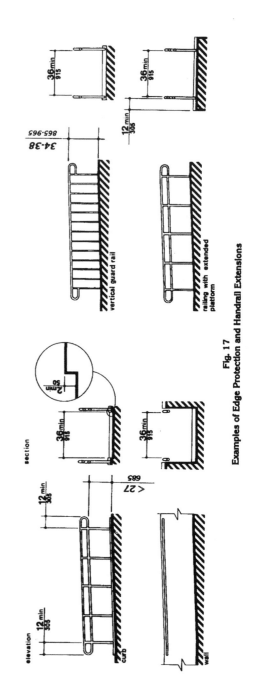

Fig. 17
Examples of Edge Protection and Handrail Extensions

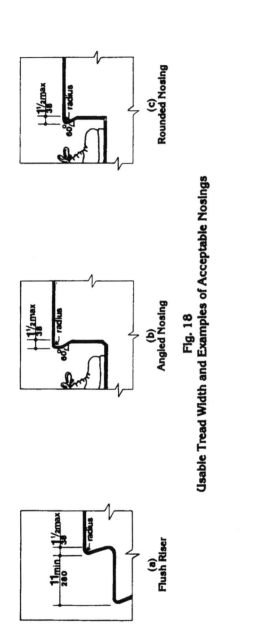

**Fig. 18
Usable Tread Width and Examples of Acceptable Nosings**

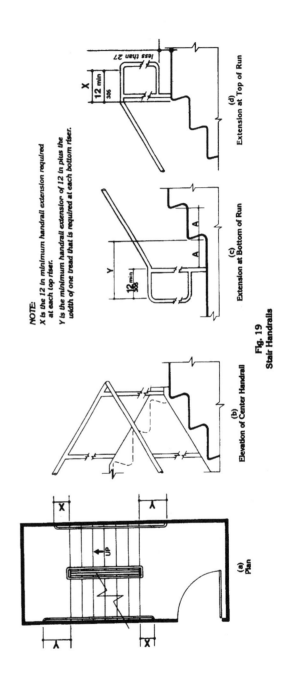

**Fig. 19
Stair Handrails**

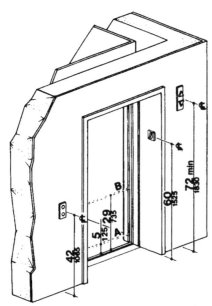

NOTE: The automatic door reopening device is activated if an object passes through either line A or line B. Line A and line B represent the vertical locations of the door reopening device not requiring contact.

Fig. 20
Hoistway and Elevator Entrances

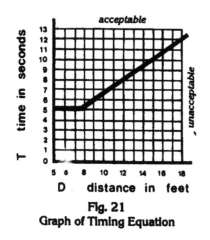

Fig. 21
Graph of Timing Equation

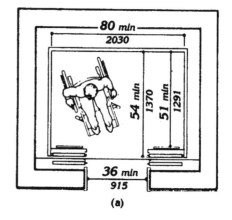

(a)

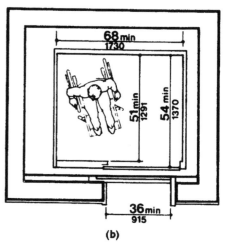

(b)

Fig. 22
Minimum Dimensions of Elevator Cars

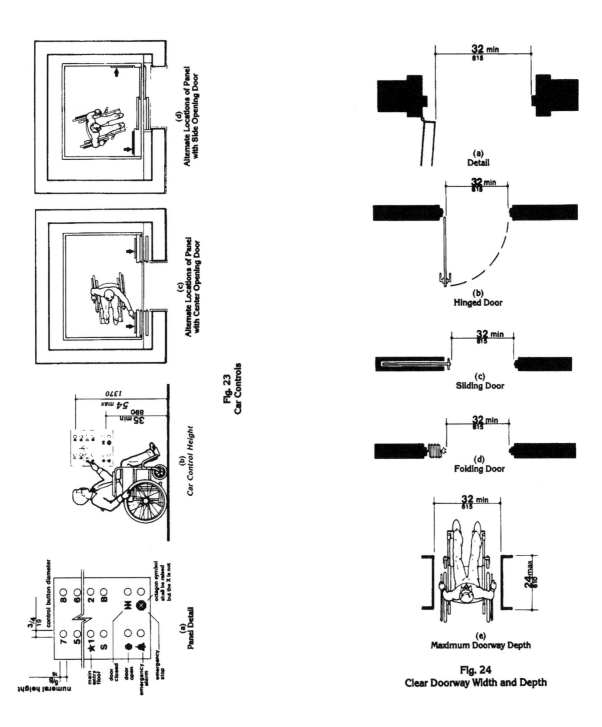

**Fig. 23
Car Controls**

**Fig. 24
Clear Doorway Width and Depth**

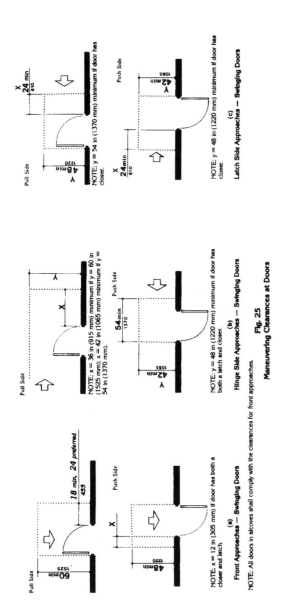

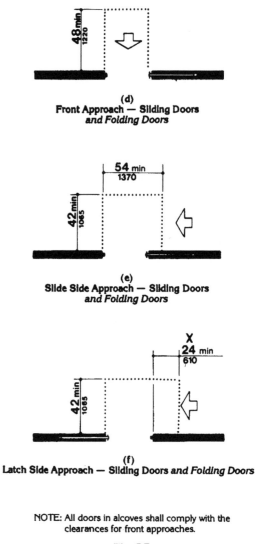

(d)
Front Approach — Sliding Doors
and Folding Doors

(e)
Slide Side Approach — Sliding Doors
and Folding Doors

(f)
Latch Side Approach — Sliding Doors *and Folding Doors*

NOTE: All doors in alcoves shall comply with the
clearances for front approaches.

Fig. 25
Maneuvering Clearances at Doors *(Continued)*

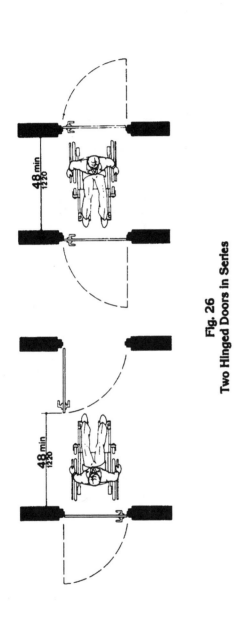

Fig. 26
Two Hinged Doors in Series

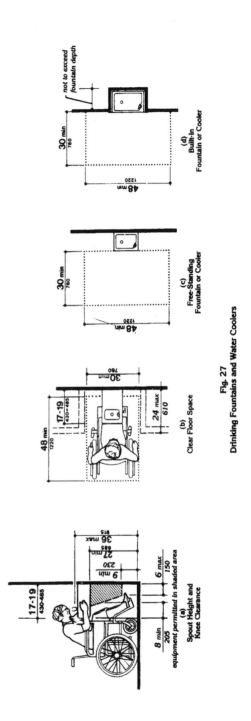

(d)
Built-in
Fountain or Cooler

(c)
Free-Standing
Fountain or Cooler

(b)
Clear Floor Space

Fig. 27
Drinking Fountains and Water Coolers

(a)
Spout Height and
Knee Clearance

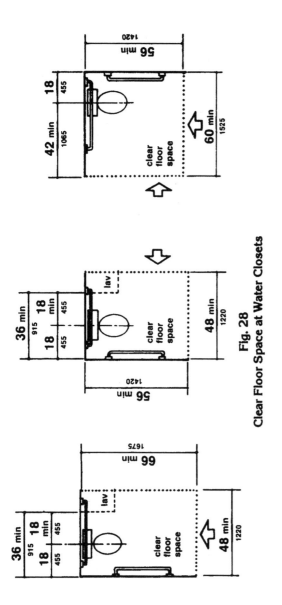

Fig. 28
Clear Floor Space at Water Closets

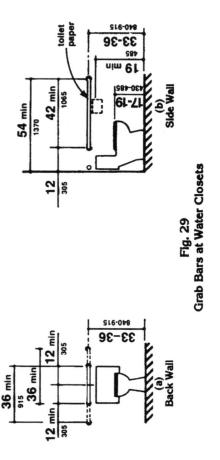

Fig. 29
Grab Bars at Water Closets

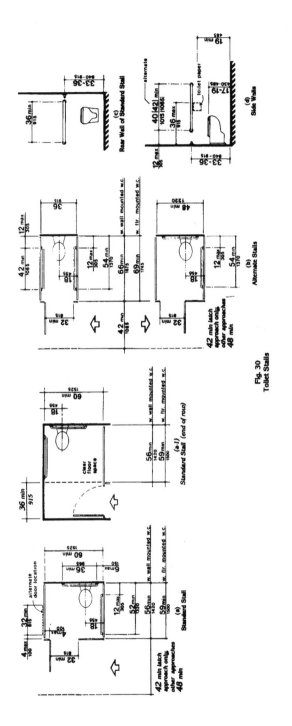

Fig. 30
Toilet Stalls

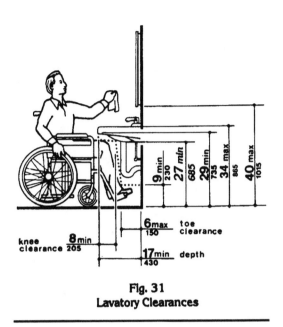

Fig. 31
Lavatory Clearances

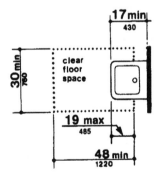

Fig. 32
Clear Floor Space at Lavatories

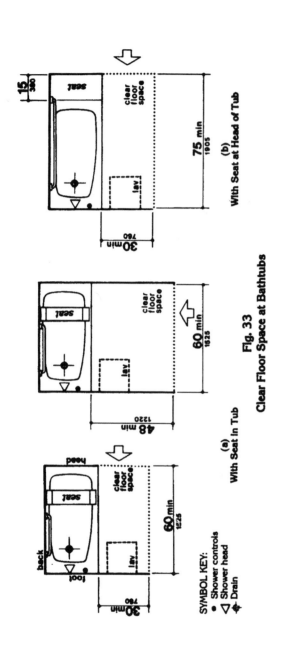

SYMBOL KEY:
- ● Shower controls
- ▽ Shower head
- ✛ Drain

Fig. 33
Clear Floor Space at Bathtubs

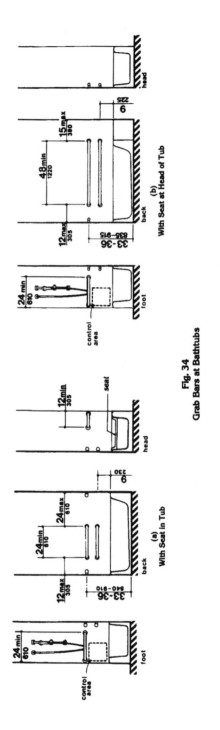

Fig. 34
Grab Bars at Bathtubs

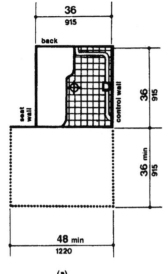

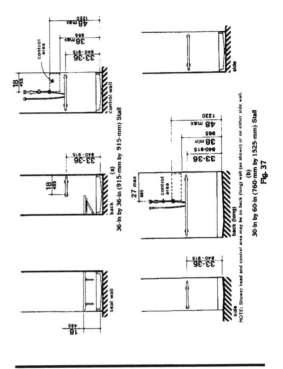

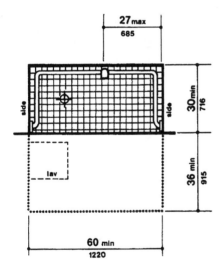

(a)
36-in by 36-in
(915-mm by 915-mm) Stall

(b)
30-in by 60-in
(760-mm by 1525-mm) Stall

Fig. 35
Shower Size and Clearances

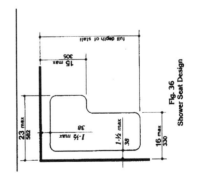

Fig. 36
Shower Seat Design

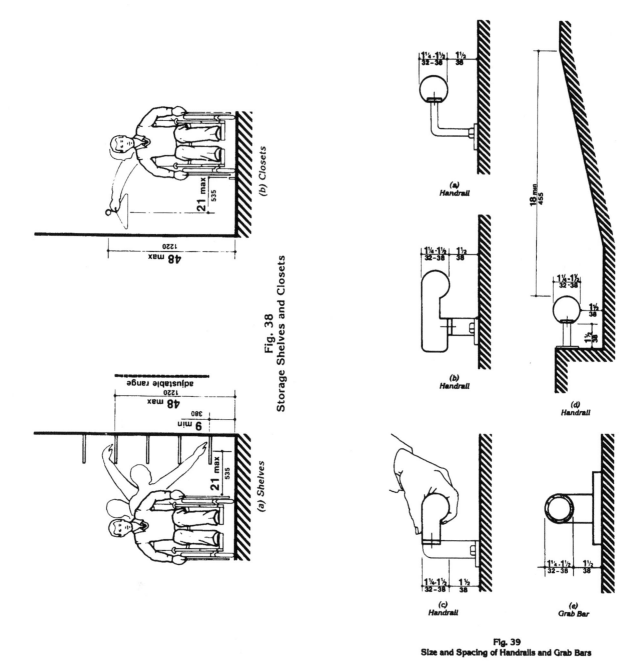

Fig. 38
Storage Shelves and Closets

Fig. 39
Size and Spacing of Handrails and Grab Bars

(a)
Proportions
International Symbol of Accessibility

(b)
Display Conditions
International Symbol of Accessibility

(c)
International TDD Symbol

(d)
International Symbol of Access for Hearing Loss

Fig. 43
International Symbols

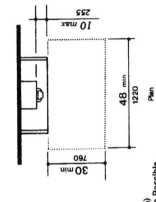

(a)
Side Reach Possible

Fig. 44
Mounting Heights and Clearances for Telephones

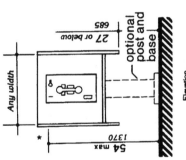

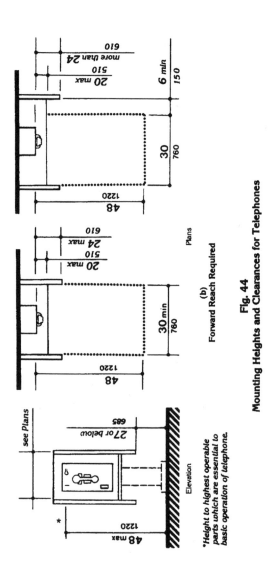

(b)
Forward Reach Required

Fig. 44
Mounting Heights and Clearances for Telephones

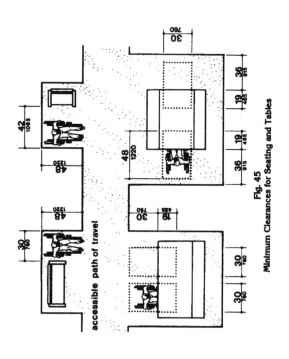

accessible path of travel

Fig. 45
Minimum Clearances for Seating and Tables

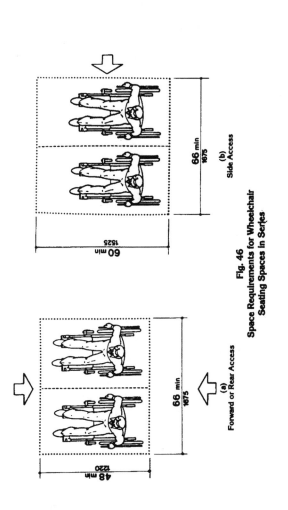

Fig. 46
Space Requirements for Wheelchair
Seating Spaces in Series

(b)
Side Access

66 min
1675

60 min
1525

(a)
Forward or Rear Access

66 min
1675

48 min
1220

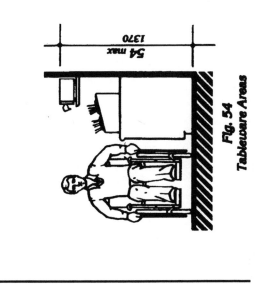

Fig. 54
Tableware Areas

54 max
1370

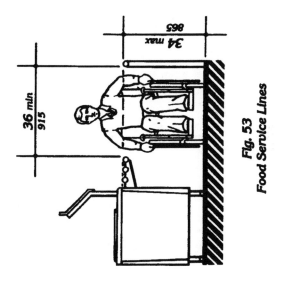

Fig. 53
Food Service Lines

34 max
865

36 min
915

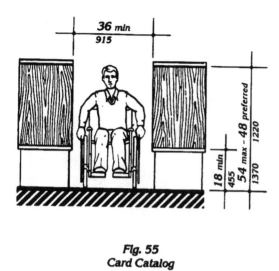

Fig. 55
Card Catalog

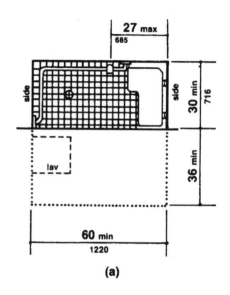

(a)

Fig. 56
Stacks

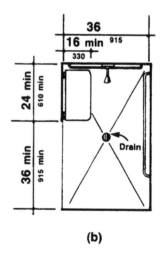

(b)

Fig. 57
Roll-in Shower with Folding Seat

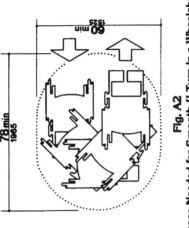

Fig. A2
Space Needed for Smooth U-Turn in a Wheelchair

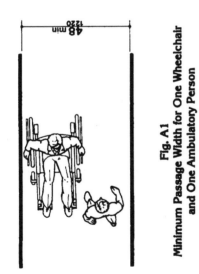

Fig. A1
Minimum Passage Width for One Wheelchair and One Ambulatory Person

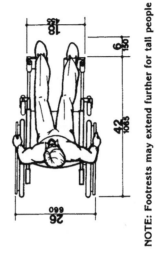

NOTE: Footrests may extend further for tall people

Fig. A3
Dimensions of Adult-Sized Wheelchairs

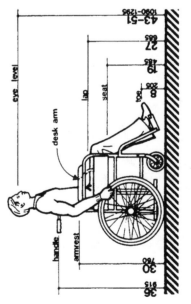

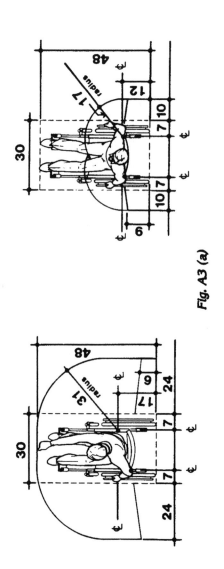

Fig. A3 (a)

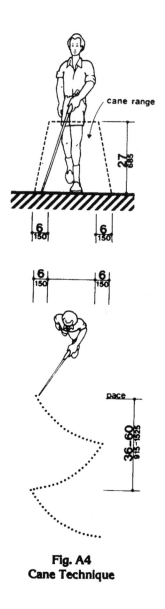

**Fig. A4
Cane Technique**

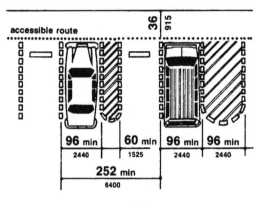

(a)
Van Accessible Space at End Row

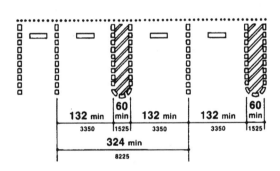

(b)
Universal Parking Space Design

Fig. A5
Parking Space Alternatives

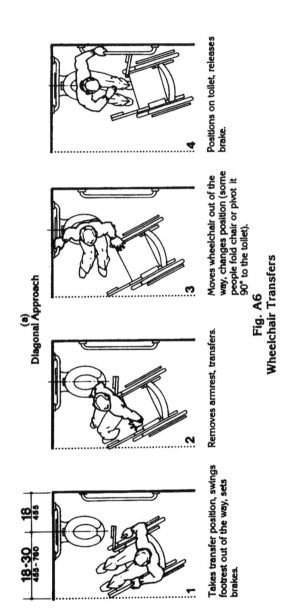

Fig. A6
Wheelchair Transfers

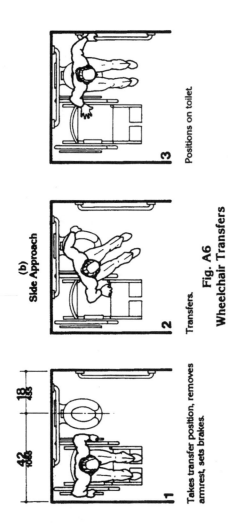

Takes transfer position, removes armrest, sets brakes.

Transfers.

Positions on toilet

(b)
Side Approach

Fig. A6
Wheelchair Transfers

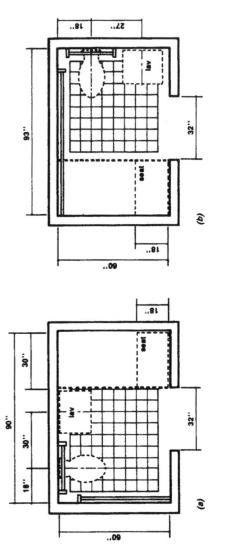

Fig. A7

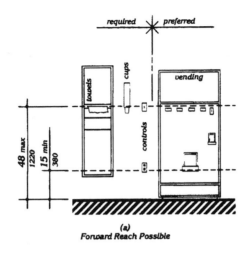

(a)
Forward Reach Possible

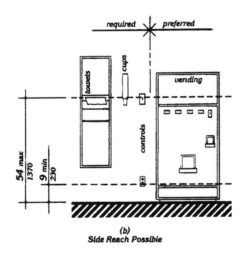

(b)
Side Reach Possible

Fig. A8
Control Reach Limitations

*   *   *

Compliance Strategies for ADA

Summary of Facilities Issues

Now that you've had a chance to learn about the history and background of ADA, what ADA is, Title II and Title III issues and an overview of the accessibility guidelines requirements, let's summarize the facilities issues and review some of the compliance strategies associated with ADA and your facilities. As we learned from our Facilities Compliance Flow Charts, the first step for most of you has already taken place—that is the awareness of the ADA anti-discrimination law. As we've covered, this law is broadly divided into major issues associated with the employment of people with disabilities and issues for accommodating people with disabilities in facilities and transportation services.

Next we learned, at least for Title III, that there are two branches on the tree of compliance. That is, compliance issues associated with new construction and compliance issues associated with existing buildings. As we noted for new construction, public accommodations and commercial facilities that have their first occupancy after January 26, 1993 must be designed to meet the ADA guidelines for that facility to be in compliance with ADA. If that building is a state or local government facility and therefore subject to Title II of ADA, it must be designed to meet ADA guidelines or UFAS.

Now that you have reviewed the requirements of the law and how that law relates to people with disabilities, you may be considering how best to implement the requirements of this law. First and foremost, if you believe yourself or your organization to be out of compliance, it would be wise for you to contact knowledgeable legal counsel for his or her recommendations.

What is presented in this workbook is not legal advice. We will discuss in this portion of the workbook, however, some recommendations for **compliance strategies for Title II and Title III as they relate to existing facilities, new facilities and alterations.**

Title II Compliance

Self-Evaluation

A public entity is required under Title II to "evaluate its current services, policies, and practices, and the effects thereof" that might be discriminatory to individuals with disabilities. The public entity is also required to provide an opportunity to interested persons including those with disabilities or organizations that represent persons with disabilities, "to participate in the self-evaluation process by submitting comments". For those public entities that employ 50 or more people, a file must be maintained for at least 3 years following the completion of the self-evaluation and be made available for public inspection. The file must include:

1. A list of interested persons consulted;

2. A description of areas examined and any problems identified;

3. A description of any modifications made.

The regulations for Title II printed in the Federal Register on July 26, 1991 state that those public entities that have already completed self-evaluation requirements under Section 504 of the Rehabilitation Act of 1973 need not repeat that portion of the self-evaluation but only review those policies and practices that were not included in the 504 evaluation or have changed. It is required that a public entity maintain in "operable working condition" all features of facilities and equipment that are required by the ADA and that they be "readily accessible to and usable by" people with disabilities.

It is critical at this point to understand that the self-evaluation is concerned with "program accessibility" and not necessarily a barrier free environment. As we mentioned before, this program accessibility concept appears to be more flexible than the "readily achievable removable of barriers" concept of Title III for existing facilities. This distinction is very important since the concept of program accessibility will allow for an administrative solution (i.e., rearrangement of schedules or facility assignments) rather than the requirement of Title III which stipulates that barriers should be removed where it is readily achievable to do so even if it would be more convenient to utilize an administrative solution. As you will recall, modifications to State and Local Governmental facilities are only required if the public entity elects not to take any other feasible option to make a program or activity accessible to persons with disabilities. It might be anticipated that many public entities would utilize the self-evaluation exercise to weigh the benefits of barrier removal vs. administrative rearrangements.

Through a grant from the federal government, self-evaluation materials are being developed by the Disability and Business Technical Assistance Centers to assist with preparing transition plans. This information may be obtained by calling 1-800-949-4ADA.

For your reference, an ADA Guide to Self-Evaluation and Transition Plans is included in the Appendix section of this book.

The National Association of College and University Business Officers of Washington, D.C. published an excellent guide to reviewing existing programs for Section 504 (Rehabilitation Act) concerns. The title of the book is Guide to Section 504 Self-Evaluation by G. Richard Biehl. Although this process was for Section 504 self-evaluation, the requirements of Title II of ADA use that process as a model. Keep in mind that for Title II the issue of existing buildings only comes into play as part of an overall approach to program accessibility. Surveying existing facilities is just a small part of the self-evaluation process. Renovation of all existing spaces to comply with ADA is not required, only the confirmation that all programs offered will have an option or location accessible to people with disabilities.

The NACUBO Guide to self-evaluation mentioned above was published as part of a Technical Assistance Program developed by the Department of Health, Education and Welfare in 1978. Some modifications may be required to the process, but as a general guide, you may use the following summary Report Form for Self-Evaluation:

Institutional Self-Evaluation
Summary Report Form

Date _____

I. Preliminary Information

Noncompliance identified:

Action to be taken:

Person responsible for completion (include telephone number):

Procedures to be followed:

Data or information required:

Schedule for completion (include individual steps):

Projected impact on the institution:

Relationship to "outside" organizations or persons—

Policy changes—

Staffing considerations—

Space or facility needs—

Communications needs—

Equipment, supply, or vehicle needs—

Cost factors—

Other considerations—

II. Interim Comments on Progress toward Completion

III. Final Information

Date action was completed _____

Action that was taken:

Relationship to "outside" organizations or persons—

Policy changes—

Staffing considerations—

Space or facility needs—

Communications needs—

Equipment, supply, or vehicle needs—

Cost factors—

Other considerations—

IV. Describe steps that will be taken to ensure that the policy, practice or procedure developed as a result of this action will be followed in the future. Describe also any steps that will be taken to monitor future action.

V. (If applicable) Describe any additional "voluntary" steps that will be taken to eliminate the effects of past discrimination.

Attach to this form any background information or other material relevant to this action

In the end, the public entity is required not only to evaluate its program accessibility, but to identify potential discrimination concerns and come up with a solution that eliminates those concerns as long as it does not fundamentally alter the nature of that program or is not an undue administrative or financial burden.

Title II Compliance Issues

Public entities are obligated to comply with the program accessibility requirements of Title II after the effective date, January 26, 1992. Where structural or physical changes to existing facilities are required, those changes must be made as quickly as possible after the effective date of January 26, 1992, but under no circumstances later than January 26, 1995.

For those public entities that employ 50 or more persons and elect to undertake physical or structural changes to their facilities to achieve program accessibility, there is a requirement under the regulations that a "transition plan" be formulated. The regulations state further that the plan shall, at a minimum:

1. Identify physical obstacles in the public entity's facilities that limit the accessibility of its programs or activities to individuals with disabilities:

2. Describe in detail the methods that will be used to make the facilities accessible;

3. Specify the schedule for taking the steps necessary to achieve compliance with this section and, if the time period of the transition period is longer than one year, identify steps that will be taken during each year of the transition period; and

4. Indicate the official responsible for implementation of the plan.

This plan must be developed by July 26, 1992 and the public entity must provide an opportunity for interested persons, including those with disabilities and the organizations representing people with disabilities to participate in the development of the plan by submitting comments. A copy of the transition plan must also be made available for public inspection after its development.

With regard to new construction and alterations to existing facilities constructed by or for the use of a public entity, compliance consists of conformance with either the Uniform Federal Accessibility Standards (UFAS) or the ADA Accessibility Guidelines (ADAAG). The regulations do state that "departures from particular requirements of those standards by the use of other methods shall be permitted when it is clearly evident that equivalent access to the facility or part of the facility is thereby provided".

To summarize the compliance strategies associated with program accessibility of public entities under Title II, we see that the first step is a self-evaluation of existing program accessibility identifying areas examined and any problems identified, and secondly, the description of modifications that are made or options that are available to eliminate the problems that were identified. With regard to new construction and alterations, public entities are required to simply design their facilities to meet the requirements of the ADAAG or the Uniform Federal Accessibility Standards to comply with the facilities accessibility requirements of Title II. Next we will move on to compliance requirements associated with public accommodations and commercial facilities.

Title III Compliance

Removal of Existing Barriers

Of the three facility type concerns found in Title III, that is existing facilities, new construction, and alterations, the requirements for compliance of **existing facilities** will probably be your greatest concern because there is no precedent for this type of compliance.

We discussed earlier that existing facilities (public accommodations) are held to a lesser standard of **"readily achievable removal of architectural and communication barriers"** whereas new construction and alterations are held to the higher standard of **"readily accessible to and usable by those with disabilities"**. Although this is true, the architects that you hire to design your new facilities and alterations almost always allow enough flexibility in design to allow them to creatively comply with the accessibility requirements of ADA. Therefore, the challenge lies in reviewing your existing facilities and determining where the architectural and communication barriers are (if there are any) and secondly, determining if the removal of those barriers is "readily achievable", that is, easily accomplishable and requiring little expense.

Your first step on the path to compliance is to set up an ADA Task Force. The task force should include the person in your organization responsible for ensuring compliance, a representative from human resources to deal with employment concerns, a representative responsible for facilities management and your legal counsel. The duty of the ADA Task Force is to develop an "implementation plan" for your organization. For more information on this first step we will look to the Title III regulations:

Although the obligation to engage in readily achievable barrier removal is clearly a continuing duty, the Department has declined to establish any independent requirement for an annual assessment or **self-evaluation**. It is best left to the public accommodations subject to Section 36.304 to establish policies to assess compliance that are appropriate to the particular circumstances faced by the wide range of public accommodations covered by the ADA. However, even in the absence of an explicit regulatory requirement for periodic self-evaluations, the Department still urges public accommodations to establish procedures for an ongoing assessment of their compliance with the ADA's barrier removal requirements. The Department recommends that this process include appropriate consultation with individuals with disabilities or organizations representing them. A serious effort at self-assessment and consultation can diminish the threat of litigation and save resources by identifying the most efficient means of providing required access.

The Department has been asked for guidance on the best means for public accommodations to comply voluntarily with this section. Such information is more appropriately part of the Department's technical assistance effort and will be forthcoming over the next several months. The Department recommends, however, the development of an **implementation plan** designed to achieve compliance with the ADA's barrier removal requirements before they become effective on January 26, 1992. Such a plan, if appropriately designed and diligently executed, could serve as evidence of a good faith effort to comply with the requirements of Section 36.104. In developing an implementation plan for readily achievable barrier removal, a public accommodation should consult with local organizations representing persons with disabilities and solicit their suggestions for cost-effective means of making individual places of public accommodation accessible. Such organizations may also be helpful in allocating scarce resources and establishing priorities. Local associations of businesses may want to encourage this process and serve as the forum for discussions on the local level between disability rights organizations and local businesses.

As the regulations state above, recognition of existing barriers is on the top of the list for your "implementation plan", so it would be wise for you to take a look at your facilities and/or to hire a consultant (an architect or an accessibility specialist) who is qualified to survey your existing facilities and have them point out the potential concerns. You will find at the end of this book a survey and analysis tool that can help understand those compliance issues that you should review at your existing facilities.

It might also be a good idea to discuss with your attorney the possibility of him or her hiring your ADA accessibility consultant to do the **surveys.** This strategy may, under the **attorney/client privilege scenario,** help shield your existing facilities survey findings from potential subpoena if your organization is sued over a non-compliance issue. A drawback to this strategy is that it might not work and would probably not suggest that your organization is putting forth a "good faith effort."

After the survey has been completed and you have identified potential non-complying elements of your facilities, they should be **prioritized** so that you may strategically coordinate the corrective work. Since the decision about which non-compliant conditions will be removed is a legal, financial and architectural decision which must be made by the building owner, it would be best to decide on priorities associated with corrective work with the input of your legal, financial and architectural consultants.

With regard to prioritizing the readily achievable removal of architectural and communication barriers, the ADA regulations suggest the following:

> Priorities—a public accommodation is urged to take measures to comply with the barrier removal requirements of this section in accordance with the following order of priorities.

> (1) First a public accommodation shall take measures to provide access to a place of public accommodation from public sidewalks, parking, or public transportation. These measures include, for example, installing an entrance ramp, widening entrances and providing accessible parking spaces.

(2) Second, a public accommodation shall take measures to provide access to those areas of place of public accommodation where goods and services are made available to the public. These measures include, for example, adjusting the layout of display racks, rearranging tables, providing Brailled or raised character signs, widening doors, providing visual alarms, and installing ramps.

(3) Third, a public accommodation shall take measures to provide access to restroom facilities. These measures include, for example, removal of obstructing furniture or vending machines, widening of doors, installation of ramps, providing accessible signage, widening of toilet stalls, and installation of grab bars.

(4) Fourth, a public accommodation shall take any other measures necessary to provide access to the goods, services, facilities, privileges, advantages, or accommodations of a place of public accommodation.

The regulations go on to state that the standard for technical compliance associated with barrier removal is as stringent as the technical standard associated with alterations. The regulations read as follows:

(1) Except as provided in paragraph (d)(2) of this section, measures taken to comply with the barrier removal requirements of this section shall comply with the applicable requirements for alterations in Section 36.402 and Sections 36.404-36.406 of this part for the element being altered. The path of travel requirements of Section 36.403 shall not apply to measures taken solely to comply with the barrier removal requirements of this section.

(2) If, as a result of compliance with the alterations requirements specified in paragraph (d)(1) of this section, the measures required to remove a barrier would not be readily achievable, a public accommodation may take other readily achievable measures to remove the barrier that do not fully comply with the specified requirements. Such measures include, for example, providing a ramp with a steeper slope or widening a doorway to a narrower width than that mandated by the alterations requirements. No measure shall be taken, however, that poses a significant risk to the health or safety of individuals with disabilities or others.

The regulations also offer the following limitation that will be especially well received by those of you in the retail industry:

> The rearrangement of temporary or movable structures, such as furniture, equipment and display racks is not readily achievable to the extent that it results in a significant loss of selling or serving space.

Again, it is important to note that corrective work and compliance with ADA, in regard to existing facilities, must be completed by January 26, 1992 or your organization will run a risk of civil suit.

In scheduling the completion of compliance activities, remember that the corrective work which has been identified from your survey may need to have construction documents prepared by an architect before a general contractor can submit a competitive bid. After acceptance of a low bid or after a negotiated contract has been approved, the work associated with correction of the problem can begin.

Alteration Strategies—Title III

All of the strategy suggestions mentioned under new construction would be applicable for **alterations** to your existing facilities. Although, not usually part of the basic services offered by most architects, you may wish to include in your Owner/Architect Agreement a provision which states that the Architect will review with the Owner his or her compliance strategy and identify those elements that are of extreme importance for compliance, such as: public restrooms, water fountains, accessible routes, and door considerations.

In addition to those strategies, it is important that you understand the concept mentioned in our discussion of the law called **disproportionality.**

Disproportionality, as you may recall, is the requirement that suggests that the accessible route or "path of travel", including restrooms, telephones, and drinking fountains, associated with the altered primary function area, would need to be renovated and brought into compliance if the cost of that compliance work to the bathrooms, restrooms, telephones, accessible route, etc. is a certain percentage of the overall cost of the alterations planned. This percentage has been identified by the U.S. Department of Justice as 20% of the overall cost of the primary function space alteration. Compliance for alterations is required if the physical alteration of the property is in progress after the effective date of **January 26, 1992.**

New Construction Strategies

The easiest requirements of ADA to understand may be the most difficult with which to comply. The new construction requirements are easiest to understand because your only requirement is to have your facilities designed to comply with the ADAAG. New construction may be the most difficult building type to comply with because there are no flexible limitations on the standards set forth in the ADAAG such as the "readily achievable" limitation for barrier removal or the limitation on alteration requirements defined by the phrase "to the maximum extent feasible".

What can you do to limit your legal exposure to civil suits with regard to ADA? It is imperative that you inform your architect that the ADA issue is of prime importance in the design of your new facilities, and you want him or her to do everything that can be done, within the scope and budget of the project, to provide you with a facility that is designed to "universally" accommodate those people who will use it. Remember "universal design" is that which allows your facilities to be used by all groups of people including children, those who use wheelchairs, those with sensory disabilities, those with cognitive disabilities, and the elderly.

As we mentioned in our discussion of existing facilities, new construction is held to the higher standard of care signified by the phrase **"readily accessible to and usable by the disabled"**. Most architects are already familiar with the ANSI standards which are very similar to the ADAAG.

Title III Checklist

ADA Facilities Compliance Strategies for Private Entities

1. TASK FORCE—Set up an interdepartmental ADA Task Force to coordinate all ADA compliance efforts for your organization.

2. STUDY—Carefully review the requirements of each applicable section of the Regulations and ADA Accessibility Guidelines (ADAAG).

3. CONSULT—Discuss your facilities' accessibility with your own employees who have disabilities and, if available, with local accessible design consultants and/or local disability support agencies. Remember, however, in consulting with

such individuals that an individual with a particular disability may not be sensitive to the needs of individuals with other disabilities.

4. ADOPT—Develop a detailed policy on accessibility for your facilities, communications, programs, services, policies, procedures, legal agreements and accommodations. Adopt it and communicate it, with implementation procedures, to all affected people.

5. NOTIFY—Discuss the requirements of the ADA with your architects, interior designers, landscape architects, facility managers, maintenance, custodial staff, public relations staff and others who affect the accessibility of your facilities.

6. REVIEW—Study all construction and remodeling projects in progress to minimize future problems with "readily achievable" barrier removal and/or failure to meet the "readily accessible" standard for those projects which are required to meet the full ADAAG.

7. REMOVE BARRIERS—Survey your existing "public accommodations" facilities to identify barriers to people with disabilities. Analyze, set priorities and remove those barriers immediately where such removal is readily achievable. Where it is not readily achievable to remove them, provide alternative methods where they are readily achievable. If all barriers cannot be removed immediately, develop a phased implementation plan for removal.

8. MAINTAIN—Assure that policies and procedures followed by custodial and maintenance staff or facility users do not reduce accessibility or create new barriers to individuals with disabilities.

9. DOCUMENT—Keep detailed records of both the plan and process you are following and your progress in removing barriers. Track costs for all items. This is your "good faith effort" defense log.

10. UPDATE—Review the accessibility of your facilities on an ongoing basis. Changes in technology, accessibility codes and guidelines may automatically upgrade the readily achievable standard, possibly requiring you to remove additional readily achievable barriers in future years.

11. MONITOR—Track all expenditures for alterations and renovations as well as for upgrades along the path of travel as required. These must be cataloged by date of expense per 36.403(h).

*　　　*　　　*

STATEMENT OF POLICY

It is the policy of this company,_____, to make our services, facilities, programs, and accommodations accessible to all people including people with disabilities.

If a disability prevents you from fully using our facility or enjoying our services and programs, we would like your input and ideas on how we can serve you better.

Please describe the nature of the problem you have encountered.

Please describe what we could do to provide better access through reasonable accommodations, auxiliary aids or services.

Please describe what we could do to provide access through alternative methods or the removal of barriers.

Name   _____

Address   _____

Phone   _____

(Instruction: To be used by a public accommodation after the facility has had architectural and communication barriers removed. A form similar to this may be used and a procedure set in place to provide an avenue for anyone with a disability to make a particular accessibility problem known. This allows the person with a disability to see that those responsible for the facility are making a good faith effort to provide access in their facility. It will, perhaps, provide a means of resolution for both parties and avoid legal action.)

Appendix

A Guide to ADA Self-Evaluation and Transition Plans

Title Two—Public Entities

Under the Americans with Disabilities Act, public entities are required to prepare self-evaluation plans to review all programs, services, activities, and benefits offered by each of their agencies, departments and instrumentalities to their own citizens and to others.

Under Section 506 of the ADA Law, the Department of Justice is required to prepare technical assistance materials to assist public entities in their efforts to comply with the requirements of the ADA. The technical assistance manuals now being prepared by DOJ for that purpose may not be available until mid to late summer of 1992. Therefore, Evan Terry Associates has prepared the attached lists to assist public entities in their understanding of the broad scope of considerations to be made in preparing these self-evaluations and to help enable entities to prepare timely responses to the July 26th deadline for completion of their transition plans. These lists are not all-inclusive nor are they completely applicable to any one entity, agency or department.

For the purpose of this document, it is assumed that the formal transition plan required by the ADA of all public entities with 50 or more employees will be developed concurrently or as a part of this process. For smaller entities, the transition plan (which looks at physical barriers) is assumed to be actually integrated into the self-evaluation plan.

Preparation of a self-evaluation plan requires the review of a significant number of factors affecting accessibility. Some of those types of considerations include:

- The administrative process followed to prepare the plan,

- The types of programs, benefits, services, activities, etc. offered or provided by the entity and/or its agencies and departments,

- Entities receiving significant assistance from the public entity preparing the self- evaluation,

- Those policies, procedures, and practices that govern the availability and administration of those programs, activities and services.

Other considerations which should be addressed in the preparation of the self-evaluation plan are: 1) administrative options for the removal of barriers, 2) exceptions to the strict requirements and 3) the breadth of the types of disabilities experienced by individual participants in the programs and covered by the ADA.

A sample administrative process:

1. Identify an ADA Coordinator for each department, agency or instrumentality under your jurisdiction. Set up an ADA Task Force to coordinate compliance efforts between those ADA Coordinators and establish quality control procedures for uniform compliance where applicable.

2. Establish policies and procedures for identifying barriers to people with disabilities within your entity and for developing and selecting options to remove those barriers. Involve people with disabilities in those efforts as members of committees, task forces, and in the review process.

3. Establish grievance procedures and assign individuals to follow up on complaints of discrimination.

4. Assign compliance responsibilities to each Coordinator. Review ADA require- ments and your compliance policies and procedures with all ADA Coordinators. Train coordinators and task force members about their responsibilities.

5. Develop a realistic schedule for completion of the self-evaluation process considering the federally-mandated deadlines (see Public Entity Timetable by ETA) and your own entity's resources. The schedule should allow for concurrent removal of physical barriers, modification of policies and other steps during the completion of the self-evaluation and transition plans. Also include time for public review and comment.

6. Begin the self-evaluation and transition planning process. Collect all relevant documents and manuals. Assess all programs, services, activities, benefits, and public facilities for barriers to people with disabilities.

7. Conduct periodic reviews with all ADA Coordinators to verify progress and work out problems. These reviews may be most productive when some are conducted in a large group setting and some are held one-on-one or in a series of small group meetings.

8. Prepare preliminary draft reports for internal review. Revise and submit draft self-evaluation and transition plans for public review and comment as scheduled. These plans should identify all forms of discrimination against individuals with disabilities and describe how discrimination will be stopped, when, and who will be responsible for implementing the changes. Modify grievance procedures as necessary to accommodate individuals who have complaints.

9. After receiving public comments, revise both the self-evaluation plan and the transition plan to include needed changes. Publish the final plans and keep them on file as required.

Documentation:

A compliant self-evaluation will include, as a minimum, 1) a list of the interested parties consulted, 2) a description of the areas examined and problems identified, and 3) a description of modifications made. If it has omitted programs evaluated under the requirements of the rehab act, those should be noted and coordinated. Any time that exclusionary policies, procedures or practices will not be modified due to one of the allowable exceptions to required compliance, provide proper and complete justification.

A compliant transition plan will include 1) a full list of physical barriers that limit program access, 2) a detailed outline of the methods which will be used to remove those barriers, 3) if full compliance will not be achieved by July 26, 1993, a schedule showing the interim steps required to achieve full compliance by January 26, 1995, and 4) the name(s) of the official(s) responsible for implementation of the plan.

Carefully document the procedures, findings and accommodations made during your entire evaluation and correction process, especially the public review and comment process. Institute follow up procedures to assure continued compliance as programs, facilities and other considerations change.

Types of programs, benefits, services, activities, etc. covered

Communications

The ADA specifies that communications by public entities must be as effective for people with disabilities as for others. This includes communications with employees, applicants for programs, participants and members of the public. That will usually mean that more than one format will be available for all communications. It may also require auxiliary aids and/or services be provided to communicate with individuals with sensory or speech impairments. Where such services or aids are required but not readily available, provisions should be made for communicating how they can be secured when needed.

Note that communications are a part of almost all programs but they may also be programs in themselves. When they are programs, they should be reviewed for how they communicate to people with various disabilities and, in some cases, to verify that they do not portray people with disabilities in an offensive or demeaning manner.

- Multisensory communications
  - Meetings
  - Performances
  - Television (broadcast and recorded)
  - Audio-visual
  - Libraries and reading rooms
  - etc.

- Visual communications
  - Written (letters, handouts, etc.)
  - Publications
  - Posted notices
  - Signage
  - etc.

- Audible communications
  - Oral
  - Public address systems
  - Radio
  - Recorded
  - Telephone and voice mail systems
  - Telephone emergency systems
  - etc.

- Electronic communications systems
  - TDD's and other telecommunication devices
  - Computer bulletin boards
  - Computer modems

- Tactile communications
  - Raised letter signage
  - Braille

- "Hands-on" programs and exhibits

Other Programs

- Education programs including schools, colleges, adult programs, continuing education programs, in-house training and correspondence programs. Events produced by or held at educational facilities for members of the public, parents and friends must also be fully accessible.

- Athletic programs and services.

- Recreational Programs, parks, improvements to lakes, beaches, facilities, etc.

- Transportation systems, routes and vehicles.

- Public walkways connecting public transportation stops to ADA-covered entities.

- Evacuation plans (during natural disasters and from buildings).

- Employment services.

- Historic preservation programs and facilities.

- Financial aid programs.

- Food service programs and facilities.

- Public assembly programs, events and facilities.

- Public housing programs and facilities.

- Counseling services.

- Healthcare programs and facilities.

- Social programs and services.

- Information services, Libraries and Reading rooms.

- Public utility benefits and services and any similar entities under the control of, or having special recognition from a public entity.

- Physical barriers in facilities where program access is blocked:
  - New construction
  - Alterations
  - Existing facilities
  - Owned and leased

- Equipment which is inaccessible. Especially equipment which is difficult for people with manual, hearing or visual impairments.

Significant assistance to private entities

The ADA says that public entities may not provided significant assistance to any entity which discriminates based on disability. Neither may a public entity, through licensure or other arrangements, follow policies which discriminate or have the effect of discriminating against people with disabilities.

- Grants

- Procurement activities

- Contracts

- Leases

- Co-sponsorships, public/private partnerships

- Licenses

Policies, procedures, practices, etc.

Policies, procedures and practices that govern the administration of programs, activities and services offered by public entities must also be evaluated to determine if they have the effect of discriminating against people with disabilities. Some examples of the types of policies would include:

- Personnel policies, practices, procedures & benefits packages including advertising or recruiting for positions, interviewing (including the facilities where applications are announced or accepted and where interviews are held), hiring, evaluating, promoting, firing, reasonable accommodations, communications, etc. (See EEO regulations for full ADA employment provisions.) Agreements with labor unions and employment agencies.

- Policy and procedure manuals for public programs.

- Advertisements and notices

- Admissions Policies such as testing, admissions criteria, interviewing, etc.

- Qualifications

- Training

- Meetings

- Scheduling

- Budgeting

- Planning and advisory boards

- Elections and voting

- Laws and Ordinances

- Regulations

- Administrative manuals and guides

- Policy directives and administrative memoranda

- Local customs which discriminate when followed by a public entity

- Methods for notifying employees, participants and beneficiaries of programs or services offered

- Selection of facilities to be used in offering programs

These items, and others, should be reviewed for the way they are developed, the way decisions are made, who is involved in those decisions, how they are revised and communicated and the impact (directly or indirectly) that they have on people with disabilities. Any criteria set up which limits participation by people with disabilities must arise from particular program needs. Files containing medical or accommodations information about people with disabilities must be kept confidential. Policies concerning drug usage must not discriminate against former drug users.

Administrative options for the removal of barriers

- Modify policies or procedures

- Revise staffing allocations

- Provide specialized training

- Provide program or service through an alternative method (such as home delivery)

- Modify admissions criteria or testing procedures

- Provide auxiliary aids and/or services such as braille materials, large print documents, in- terpreters or readers to individuals with disabilities to assist w/communication

- Relocate program to an accessible facility (or be ready to relocate if needed)

- Remove physical barriers in existing facilities

- Construct a new, accessible facility

- Modify, redesign or purchase new, accessible equipment

- Use accessible rolling stock or other conveyances

- Other administrative methods

Exceptions

Barriers to individuals with disabilities are not required to be removed when such removal will create undue financial and administrative burdens, will fundamentally alter the nature of the program offered, result in a direct threat to others or, in some cases, alter a historic structure. Specific justifications and procedures have been outlined in the ADA regulations that must be followed properly and expeditiously when claiming any of these exceptions.

Types of disabilities covered by the ADA

Physical Disabilities

- Sensory
  - Blindness or visual impairment
  - Deafness or hearing impairment
  - Speech impairment
  - Impaired sense of touch
  - Impaired sense of smell or taste

- Motor
  - Reduced strength in fingers, limbs, head or body
  - Loss of motor function in fingers, limbs, head or body
  - Reduced endurance
  - Loss of, or reduced, motor control

Mental Disabilities

- Cognitive

- Emotional

- Psychological

- Assumed disability or history of a disability

- Association with an individual with a known disability

This list of types of disabilities is not exhaustive but is intended only to show the general range of disabilities covered by the ADA to assist public entities in their program review process.

Program Evaluation Worksheet

Program, Service, Benefit or Activity Provided by Public Entity: _____

_____

_____

Administered by: _____

    At (facility, if applicable): _____

Barrier: _____

_____

_____

_____

Possible options for correction: _____

_____

_____

_____

_____

Interested parties consulted: _____

_____

_____

Decision: _____

_____

_____

Exceptions:

Exceptions to barrier removal (by some method) are only allowed in cases where:
1. Removal would create an undue administrative and financial burden for the public entity,
2. Removal would fundamentally alter the nature of the program provided,
3. Removal would threaten the safety of others, or,
4. Removal would significantly alter the historic significance of an historic structure that has preservation of that historic property as a primary purpose.

When exceptions are taken, the final decision must be made by a department head level person and the decision and justification must be made in writing. The entire budget for a program must be considered in any decision to consider the impact of a particular barrier's removal as creating an undue administrative and financial burden. Alternative methods, if available, must be used to remove barriers where exceptions are taken.

Physical Barrier Removal Required: _____

ADA Self-Evaluation Guide / ©1992 / Evan Terry Associates, P.C. / 2129 Montgomery Highway / Birmingham, Alabama 35209 / (205) 871-9818

Transition Plan—Field Notes

Facility: _____

Location of barrier: _____

    Plan reference mark:_____ n/a _____ Photograph no:_____ n/a _____

Condition: _____

_____

_____

_____

_____

_____

_____

ADA standard referenced: _____ See sketch no:_____ n/a _____

Possible options for correction: _____

_____

_____

_____

_____

_____

Severity:
    A = Safety hazard
    B = Blocks access
    C = Major inconvenience
    D = Minor inconvenience

Location Code:
    1 = From transportation into entrance
    2 = Entrance to location where program is offered
    3 = Toilets
    4 = All other public areas
    5 = Employee areas

               Severity:_____

       Location code:_____

Decision: _____

_____

_____

_____

            Remove physical barrier:_____

ADA Self-Evaluation Guide / ©1992 / Evan Terry Associates, P.C. / 2129 Montgomery Highway / Birmingham, Alabama 35209 / (205) 871-9818

Checklist for Existing Facilities

The Americans with Disabilities Act Survey for Readily Achievable Barrier Removal

**Developed under a grant from the National
Institute on Disability and Rehabilitation
Research by Adaptive Environments Center, Inc.
and Barrier Free Environments, Inc.**

© 1992

*Also available from your Disability and
Business Technical Assistance Center:*

Fact Sheet 1. What is a Public Accommodation?
Fact Sheet 2. Auxiliary Aids and Services
Fact Sheet 3. Communicating with People with Disabilities
Fact Sheet 4. Tax Incentives for Accessibility Improvements
Fact Sheet 5. Alternatives to Barrier Removal
Fact Sheet 6. Resources for More Information

*To obtain additional copies of this checklist, contact your
Disability and Business Technical Assistance Center.
To find out the name and number of your regional center,
call (617) 349-2639, or refer to Fact Sheet 6.*

*Adaptive Environments Center, Inc. and Barrier Free
Environments, Inc. are authorized by the National Institute on
Disability and Rehabilitation Research (NIDRR) to provide
information, materials, and technical assistance to individuals
and entities that are covered by the Americans with Disabilities
Act (ADA). However, you should be aware that NIDRR is
not responsible for enforcement of the ADA. The information,
materials, and/or technical assistance are intended solely as
informal guidance, and are neither a determination of your legal
rights or responsibilities under the Act, nor binding on any
agency with enforcement responsibility under the ADA.*

The Americans with Disabilities Act

This document was produced with funding under a grant from the National Institute on Disability and Rehabilitation Research for distribution at no charge to the public through the Disability and Business Technical Assistance Centers. For further information, call 1-800-949-4ADA. It is reprinted here for your convenience.

Checklist for Existing Facilities

Introduction

Title III of the Americans with Disabilities Act requires public accommodations to provide goods and services to people with disabilities on an equal basis with the rest of the general public. The goal is to afford every individual the opportunity to benefit from our country's businesses and services, and to afford our businesses and services the opportunity to benefit from the patronage of all Americans.

By **January 26, 1992**, architectural and communication barriers must be removed in public areas of **existing facilities** when their removal is **readily achievable**—in other words, easily accomplished and able to be carried out without much difficulty or expense. **Public accommodations** that must meet the barrier removal requirement include a broad range of establishments (both for-profit and nonprofit)—such as hotels, restaurants, theaters, museums, retail stores, private schools, banks, doctors' offices, and other places that serve the public. People who own, lease, lease out, or operate places of public accommodation in existing buildings are responsible for complying with the barrier removal requirement.

The removal of barriers can often be achieved by making simple changes to the physical environment. However, the regulations do not define exactly how much effort and expense are required for a facility to meet its obligation. This judgment must be made on a case-by-case basis, taking into consideration such factors as the size, type, and overall financial resources of the facility, and the nature and cost of the access improvements needed. These factors are described in more detail in the ADA regulations issued by the Department of Justice.

The process of determining what changes are readily achievable is not a one-time effort; access should be re-evaluated annually. Barrier removal that might be difficult to carry out now may be readily achievable later. Tax incentives are available to help absorb costs over several years.

Purpose of this Checklist

This checklist will help you identify accessibility problems and solutions in existing facilities in order to meet your obligations under the ADA.

The goal of the survey process is to plan how to make an existing facility more usable for people with disabilities. The Department of Justice recommends the development of an Implementation Plan, specifying what improvements you will make to remove barriers and when each solution will be carried out: "...Such a plan...could serve as evidence of a good faith effort to comply...."

Technical Requirements

This checklist details some of the requirements found in the ADA Accessibility Guidelines (ADAAG). However, keep in mind that **full compliance with ADAAG is required only for new construction and alterations. The requirements are presented here as a guide to help you determine what may be readily achievable barrier removal for existing facilities.** Whenever possible, ADAAG should be used in making readily achievable modifications. If complying with ADAAG is not readily achievable, you may undertake a modification that does not fully comply with ADAAG using less stringent standards, as long as it poses no health or safety risk.

Each state has its own regulations regarding accessibility. To ensure compliance with all codes, know your state and local codes and use the more stringent technical requirement for every modification you make; that is, the requirement that provides greater access for individuals with disabilities. The barrier removal requirement for existing facilities is new under the ADA and supersedes less stringent local or state codes.

What this Checklist is *Not*

This checklist does not cover all of ADAAG's requirements; therefore, it is not for facilities undergoing new construction or alterations. In addition, it does not attempt to illustrate all possible barriers or propose all possible barrier removal solutions. ADAAG should be consulted for guidance in situations not covered here.

The checklist does not cover Title III's requirements for nondiscriminatory policies and practices and for the provision of auxiliary communication aids and services. The communication features covered are those that are structural in nature.

Priorities

This checklist is based on the four priorities recommended by the Title III regulations for planning readily achievable barrier removal projects:

Priority 1: Accessible entrance into the facility
Priority 2: Access to goods and services
Priority 3: Access to rest rooms
Priority 4: Any other measures necessary

How to Use this Checklist

√ **Get Organized:** Establish a time frame for completing the survey. Determine how many copies of the checklist you will need to survey the whole facility. Decide who will conduct the survey. It is strongly recommended, particularly for large facilities, that you invite two or three additional people, including people with various disabilities, to assist in identifying barriers, developing solutions for removing these barriers, and setting priorities for implementing improvements.

√ **Obtain Floor Plans:** It is very helpful to have the building floor plans with you while you survey. If plans are not available, use graph paper to sketch the layout of all interior and exterior spaces used by your organization. Make notes on the sketch or plan while you are surveying.

√ **Conduct the Survey:** Bring copies of this checklist, a clipboard, a pencil or pen, and a flexible

steel tape measure. With three people surveying, one person numbers key items on the floor plan to match with the field notes, taken by a second person, while the third takes measurements. Think about each space from the perspective of people with physical, hearing, visual, and cognitive disabilities, noting areas that need improvement.

√ **Summarize Barriers and Solutions:** List barriers found and ideas for their removal. Consider the solutions listed beside each question, and add your own ideas. Consult with building contractors and equipment suppliers to estimate the costs for making the proposed modifications.

√ **Make Decisions and Set Priorities:** Review the summary with decision makers and advisors. Decide which solutions will best eliminate barriers at a reasonable cost. Prioritize the items you decide upon and make a timeline for carrying them out. Where the removal of barriers is not readily achievable, you must consider whether there are alternative methods for providing access that are readily achievable.

√ **Maintain Documentation:** Keep your survey, notes, summary, record of work completed, and plans for alternative methods on file.

√ **Make Changes:** Implement changes as planned. Always refer directly to ADAAG and your state and local codes for complete technical requirements before making any access improvement. References to the applicable sections of ADAAG are listed at the beginning of each group of questions. If you need help understanding the federal, state or local requirements, contact your Disability and Business Technical Assistance Center.

√ **Follow Up:** Review your Implementation Plan each year to re-evaluate whether more improvements have become readily achievable.

To obtain a copy of the ADAAG or other information from the U.S. Department of Justice, call: (202) 514-0301 Voice, (202) 514-0381 TT, (202) 514-0383 TT. For technical questions, contact the Architectural and Transportation Barriers Compliance Board at (800) USA-ABLE.

2

| QUESTIONS | POSSIBLE SOLUTIONS |

Priority 1:
Accessible Entrance

People with disabilities should be able to arrive on the site, approach the building, and enter the building as freely as everyone else. At least one path of travel should be safe and accessible for everyone, including people with disabilities.

Yes No

Path of Travel (ADAAG 4.3, 4.4, 4.5, 4.7)
Is there a path of travel that does not require the use of stairs? ☐ ☐

☐ Add a ramp if the path of travel is interrupted by stairs.
☐ Add an alternative pathway on level ground.

Is the path of travel stable, firm and slip-resistant? ☐ ☐

☐ Repair uneven paving.
☐ Fill small bumps and breaks with beveled patches.
☐ Replace gravel with hard top.

Is the path at least 36 inches wide? ☐ ☐

☐ Change or move landscaping, furnishings, or other features that narrow the path of travel.
☐ Widen pathway.

Can all objects protruding into the path be detected by a person with a visual disability using a cane? ☐ ☐

☐ Move or remove protruding objects.
☐ Add a cane-detectable base that extends to the ground.
☐ Place a cane-detectable object on the ground underneath as a warning barrier.

In order to be detected using a cane, an object must be within 27 inches of the ground. Objects hanging or mounted overhead must be higher than 80 inches to provide clear head room. It is not necessary to remove objects that protrude less than 4 inches from the wall.

Do curbs on the pathway have curb cuts at drives, parking, and drop-offs? ☐ ☐

☐ Install curb cut.
☐ Add small ramp up to curb.

Ramps (ADAAG 4.8)
Are the slopes of ramps no greater than 1:12? ☐ ☐

☐ Lengthen ramp to decrease slope.
☐ Relocate ramp.
☐ If available space is limited, reconfigure ramp to include switchbacks.

Slope is given as a ratio of the height to the length. 1:12 means for every 12 inches along the base of the ramp, the height increases one inch. For a 1:12 maximum slope, at least one foot of ramp length is needed for each inch of height.

1 : 12

3

Checklist for Existing Facilities   Adaptive Environments Center and Barrier Free Environments

QUESTIONS			POSSIBLE SOLUTIONS

	Yes	No	

Ramps, continued

Do all ramps longer than 6 feet have railings on both sides? □ □ — □ Add railings.

Are railings sturdy, and between 34 and 38 inches high? □ □ — □ Adjust height of railings. / □ Secure handrails.

Is the width between railings at least 36 inches? □ □ — □ Relocate the railings. / □ Widen the ramp.

Are ramps non-slip? □ □ — □ Add non-slip surface material.

Is there a 5-foot-long level landing at every 30-foot horizontal length of ramp, at the top and bottom of ramps and at switchbacks? □ □ — □ Remodel or relocate ramp.

The ramp should rise no more than 30 inches between landings.

Parking and Drop-Off Areas (ADAAG 4.6)

Are an adequate number of accessible parking spaces available (8 feet wide for car plus 5-foot striped access aisle)? For guidance in determining the appropriate number to designate, the table below gives the ADAAG requirements for new construction and alterations (for lots with more than 100 spaces, refer to ADAAG): □ □ — □ Reconfigure a reasonable number of spaces by repainting stripes.

Total spaces	Accessible
1 to 25	1 space
26 to 50	2 spaces
51 to 75	3 spaces
76 to 100	4 spaces

Are 16-foot-wide spaces, with 98 inches of vertical clearance, available for lift-equipped vans? □ □ — □ Reconfigure to provide a reasonable number of van-accessible spaces.

At least one of every 8 accessible spaces must be van-accessible.

Are the accessible spaces closest to the accessible entrance? □ □ — □ Reconfigure spaces.

Are accessible spaces marked with the International Symbol of Accessibility? Are there signs reading "Van Accessible" at van spaces? □ □ — □ Add signs, placed so that they are not obstructed by cars.

International Symbol of Accessibility:

4

Checklist for Existing Facilities   Adaptive Environments Center and Barrier Free Environments

QUESTIONS	POSSIBLE SOLUTIONS

Yes   No

Parking and Drop-Off Areas, continued
Is there an enforcement procedure to ensure
that accessible parking is used only by those
who need it?

☐ Implement a policy to check peri-
odically for violators and report
them to the proper authorities.

Entrance (ADAAG 4.13, 4.14)
If there are stairs at the main entrance, is there
also a ramp or lift, or is there an alternative
accessible entrance?

> **Do not use a service entrance as the
> accessible entrance** unless there is no
> other option.

☐ If it is not possible to make
the main entrance accessible,
create a dignified alternate
accessible entrance. Make sure
there is accessible parking near
accessible entrances.

Do all inaccessible entrances have signs indicating the location of the nearest accessible entrance?

☐ Install signs at or before
inaccessible entrances.

Can the alternate accessible entrance be used
independently?

☐ Eliminate as much as possible
the need for assistance—to answer
a doorbell, to operate a lift, or to
put down a temporary ramp,
for example.

Does the entrance door have at least 32 inches
clear opening (for a double door, at least one
32-inch leaf)?

☐ Widen the door.
☐ Install offset (swing-clear) hinges.

Is there at least 18 inches of clear wall space on
the pull side of the door, next to the handle?

> **A person using a wheelchair** needs this
> space to get close enough to open the door.

☐ Remove or relocate furnishings,
partitions, or other obstructions.
☐ Move door.
☐ Add power-assisted door opener.

Is the threshold level (less than 1/4 inch) or
beveled, up to 1/2 inch high?

☐ If there is a single step with a rise
of 6 inches or less, add a short ramp.
☐ If there is a high threshold, remove
it or add a bevel.

Are doormats 1/2 inch high or less, and
secured to the floor at all edges?

☐ Replace or remove mats.
☐ Secure mats at edges.

Is the door handle no higher than 48 inches and
operable with a closed fist?

> **The "closed fist" test for handles and
> controls:** Try opening the door or operat-
> ing the control using only one hand, held
> in a fist. If you can do it, so can a person
> who has limited use of his or her hands.

☐ Replace inaccessible knob with a
lever or loop handle.
☐ Retrofit with an add-on lever
extension.

5

🏳 **ADA Facilities Compliance**™
7-92

Checklist for Existing Facilities　　　**Adaptive Environments Center and Barrier Free Environments**

QUESTIONS	POSSIBLE SOLUTIONS

	Yes	No	
Entrance, continued Can doors be opened without too much force (maximum is 5 lbf)? **You can use a fish scale** to measure the force required to open a door. Attach the hook of the scale to the doorknob or handle. Pull on the ring end of the scale until the door opens, and read off the amount of force required. If you do not have a fish scale, you will need to judge subjectively whether the door is easy enough to open.	☐	☐	☐ Adjust the door closers and oil the hinges. ☐ Install power-assisted door openers. ☐ Install lighter doors.
If the door has a closer, does it take at least 3 seconds to close?	☐	☐	☐ Adjust door closer.
Emergency Egress (ADAAG 4.28) Do all alarms have both flashing lights and audible signals?	☐	☐	☐ Install visible and audible alarms.
Is there sufficient lighting in egress pathways such as stairs, corridors, and exits?	☐	☐	☐ Upgrade, add, or clean bulbs or fixtures.

Priority 2:
Access to Goods and Services

Ideally, the layout of the building should allow people with disabilities to obtain goods or services without special assistance. Where it is not possible to provide full accessibility, assistance or alternative services should be available upon request.

	Yes	No	
Horizontal Circulation (ADAAG 4.3) Does the accessible entrance provide direct access to the main floor, lobby, or elevator?	☐	☐	☐ Add ramps or lifts. ☐ Make another entrance accessible.
Are all public spaces on an accessible path of travel?	☐	☐	☐ Provide access to all public spaces along an accessible path of travel.
Is the accessible route to all public spaces at least 36 inches wide?	☐	☐	☐ Move furnishings such as tables, chairs, display racks, vending machines, and counters to make more room.
Is there a 5-foot circle or a T-shaped space for a person using a wheelchair to reverse direction?	☐	☐	☐ Rearrange furnishings, displays, and equipment.

6

Checklist for Existing Facilities   Adaptive Environments Center and Barrier Free Environments

QUESTIONS	POSSIBLE SOLUTIONS

Yes   No

Doors (ADAAG 4.13)
Do doors into public spaces have at least a 32-inch clear opening?

☐ Install offset (swing-clear) hinges.
☐ Widen doors.

On the pull side of doors, next to the handle, is there at least 18 inches of clear wall space so that a person using a wheelchair can get near to open the door?

☐ Reverse the door swing if it is safe to do so.
☐ Move or remove obstructing partitions.

Can doors be opened without too much force (5 lbf maximum)?

☐ Adjust or replace closers.
☐ Install lighter doors.
☐ Install power-assisted door openers.

Are door handles 48 inches high or less and operable with a closed fist?

☐ Lower handles.
☐ Replace inaccessible knobs or latches with lever or loop handles.
☐ Retrofit with add-on lever extensions.
☐ Install power-assisted door openers.

Are all thresholds level (less than 1/4 inch), or beveled, up to 1/2 inch high?

☐ Remove thresholds.
☐ Add bevels to both sides.

Rooms and Spaces (ADAAG 4.2, 4.4, 4.5, 4.30)
Are all aisles and pathways to all goods and services at least 36 inches wide?

☐ Rearrange furnishings and fixtures to clear aisles.

Is there a 5-foot circle or T-shaped space for turning a wheelchair completely?

☐ Rearrange furnishings to clear more room.

Is carpeting low-pile, tightly woven, and securely attached along edges?

☐ Secure edges on all sides.
☐ Replace carpeting.

In routes through public areas, are all obstacles cane-detectable (located within 27 inches of the floor or protruding less than 4 inches from the wall), or are they higher than 80 inches?

☐ Remove obstacles.
☐ Install furnishings, planters, or other cane-detectable barriers underneath the obstacle.

Do signs designating permanent rooms and spaces, such as rest room signs, exit signs, and room numbers, comply with the appropriate requirements for accessible signage?

☐ Provide signage that has raised and brailled letters, complies with finish and contrast standards, and is mounted at the correct height and location.

7

Checklist for Existing Facilities   Adaptive Environments Center and Barrier Free Environments

QUESTIONS			POSSIBLE SOLUTIONS
	Yes	No	

Controls (ADAAG 4.27)
Are all controls that are available for use by the public (including electrical, mechanical, window, cabinet, game, and self-service controls) located at an accessible height?   ☐ ☐

☐ Relocate controls.

Reach ranges: The maximum height for a side reach is 54 inches; for a forward reach, 48 inches. The minimum reachable height is 15 inches.

Are they operable with a closed fist?   ☐ ☐

☐ Replace controls.

Seats, Tables, and Counters (ADAAG 4.2, 4.32)
Are the aisles between chairs or tables at least 36 inches wide?   ☐ ☐

☐ Rearrange chairs or tables to provide 36-inch aisles.

Are the spaces for wheelchair seating distributed throughout?   ☐ ☐

☐ Rearrange tables to allow room for wheelchairs in seating areas throughout the area.
☐ Remove some fixed seating.

Are the tops of tables or counters between 28 and 34 inches high?   ☐ ☐

☐ Lower at least a section of high tables and counters.

Are knee spaces at accessible tables at least 27 inches high, 30 inches wide, and 19 inches deep?   ☐ ☐

☐ Replace or raise tables.

Vertical Circulation (ADAAG 4.3)
Are there ramps or elevators to all levels?   ☐ ☐

☐ Install ramps or lifts.
☐ Modify a service elevator.
☐ Relocate goods or services to an accessible area.

On each level, if there are stairs between the entrance and/or elevator and essential public areas, is there an accessible alternate route?   ☐ ☐

☐ Post clear signs directing people along an accessible route to ramps, lifts, or elevators.

Stairs (ADAAG 4.9)
Do treads have a non-slip surface?   ☐ ☐

☐ Add non-slip surface to treads.

Do stairs have continuous rails on both sides, with extensions beyond the top and bottom stairs?   ☐ ☐

☐ Add or replace handrails.

8

Checklist for Existing Facilities   **Adaptive Environments Center and Barrier Free Environments**

QUESTIONS			POSSIBLE SOLUTIONS
	Yes	No	

Elevators (ADAAG 4.10)
Are there both visible and verbal or audible door opening/closing and floor indicators (one tone = up, two tones = down)?
☐ Yes ☐ No

☐ Install visible and verbal or audible signals.

Are the call buttons in the hallway no higher than 42 inches?
☐ Yes ☐ No

☐ Lower call buttons.
☐ Provide a permanently attached reach stick.

Do the controls outside and inside the cab have raised and braille lettering?
☐ Yes ☐ No

☐ Install raised lettering and braille next to buttons.

Is there a sign on the jamb at each floor identifying the floor in raised and braille letters?
☐ Yes ☐ No

☐ Install tactile signs to identify floor numbers, at a height of 60 inches from floor.

Is the emergency intercom usable without voice communication?
☐ Yes ☐ No

☐ Replace communication system.

Are there braille and raised-letter instructions for the communication system?
☐ Yes ☐ No

☐ Add simple tactile instructions.

Lifts (ADAAG 4.2, 4.11)
Can the lift be used without assistance? If not, is a call button provided?
☐ Yes ☐ No

☐ At each stopping level, post clear instructions for use of the lift.
☐ Provide a call button.

Is there at least 30 by 48 inches of clear space for a person using a wheelchair to approach to reach the controls and use the lift?
☐ Yes ☐ No

☐ Rearrange furnishings and equipment to clear more space.

Are controls between 15 and 48 inches high (up to 54 inches if a side approach is possible)?
☐ Yes ☐ No

☐ Move controls.

Priority 3:
Usability of Rest Rooms

When rest rooms are open to the public, they should be accessible to people with disabilities. Closing a rest room that is currently open to the public is not an allowable option.

Getting to the Rest Rooms (ADAAG 4.1)
If rest rooms are available to the public, is at least one rest room (either one for each sex, or unisex) fully accessible?
☐ Yes ☐ No

☐ Reconfigure rest room.
☐ Combine rest rooms to create one unisex accessible rest room.

9

Checklist for Existing Facilities   Adaptive Environments Center and Barrier Free Environments

QUESTIONS			POSSIBLE SOLUTIONS

	Yes	No	
Getting to the Rest Rooms, continued Are there signs at inaccessible rest rooms that give directions to accessible ones?	☐	☐	☐ Install accessible signs.
Doorways and Passages (ADAAG 4.2, 4.13) Is there tactile signage identifying rest rooms? **Mount signs on the wall**, on the latch side of the door. Avoid using ambiguous symbols in place of text to identify rest rooms.	☐	☐	☐ Add accessible signage, placed to the side of the door (not on the door itself). ☐ If symbols are used, add supplementary verbal signage.
Is the doorway at least 32 inches clear?	☐	☐	☐ Install offset (swing-clear) hinges. ☐ Widen the doorway.
Are doors equipped with accessible handles (operable with a closed fist), 48 inches high or less?	☐	☐	☐ Lower handles. ☐ Replace inaccessible knobs or latches with lever or loop handles. ☐ Add lever extensions. ☐ Install power-assisted door openers.
Can doors be opened easily (5 lbf maximum force)?	☐	☐	☐ Adjust or replace closers. ☐ Install lighter doors. ☐ Install power-assisted door openers.
Does the entry configuration provide adequate maneuvering space for a person using a wheelchair? **A person using a wheelchair** needs 36 inches of clear width for forward movement, and a 5-foot diameter clear space or a T-shaped space to make turns.	☐	☐	☐ Rearrange furnishings such as chairs and trash cans. ☐ Remove inner door if there is a vestibule with two doors. ☐ Move or remove obstructing partitions.
Is there a 36-inch-wide path to all fixtures?	☐	☐	☐ Remove obstructions.
Stalls (ADAAG 4.17) Is the stall door operable with a closed fist, inside and out?	☐	☐	☐ Replace inaccessible knobs with lever or loop handles. ☐ Add lever extensions.
Is there a wheelchair-accessible stall that has an area of at least 5 feet by 5 feet, clear of the door swing, OR is there a stall that is less accessible but that provides greater access than a typical stall (either 36 by 69 inches or 48 by 69 inches)?	☐	☐	☐ Move or remove partitions. ☐ Reverse the door swing if it is safe to do so.

10

Checklist for Existing Facilities   Adaptive Environments Center and Barrier Free Environments

QUESTIONS			POSSIBLE SOLUTIONS

Stalls, continued

	Yes	No	
In the accessible stall, are there grab bars behind and on the side wall nearest to the toilet?	☐	☐	☐ Add grab bars.
Is the toilet seat 17 to 19 inches high?	☐	☐	☐ Add raised seat.

Lavatories (ADAAG 4.19, 4.24)

Does one lavatory have a 30-inch-wide by 48-inch-deep clear space in front? ☐ ☐

☐ Rearrange furnishings.
☐ Replace lavatory.
☐ Remove or alter cabinetry to provide space underneath. Make sure hot pipes are insulated.

A maximum of 19 inches of the required depth may be under the lavatory.

☐ Move a partition or wall.

Is the lavatory rim no higher than 34 inches? ☐ ☐   ☐ Adjust or replace lavatory.

Is there at least 29 inches from the floor to the bottom of the lavatory apron (excluding pipes)? ☐ ☐   ☐ Adjust or replace lavatory.

Can the faucet be operated with one closed fist? ☐ ☐   ☐ Replace faucet handles with paddle type.

Are soap and other dispensers and hand dryers 48 inches high or less and usable with one closed fist? ☐ ☐
☐ Lower dispensers.
☐ Replace with or provide additional accessible dispensers.

Is the mirror mounted with the bottom edge of the reflecting surface 40 inches high or lower? ☐ ☐
☐ Lower or tilt down the mirror.
☐ Replace with larger mirror.

Priority 4:
Additional Access

When amenities such as public telephones and drinking fountains are provided to the general public, they should also be accessible to people with disabilities.

Drinking Fountains (ADAAG 4.15)

Is there at least one fountain with clear floor space of at least 30 by 48 inches in front? ☐ ☐

☐ Clear more room by rearranging or removing furnishings.

Is there one fountain with its spout no higher than 36 inches from the ground, and another with a standard height spout (or a single "hi-lo" fountain)? ☐ ☐

☐ Provide cup dispensers for fountains with spouts that are too high.
☐ Provide an accessible water cooler.

11

Checklist for Existing Facilities

QUESTIONS			POSSIBLE SOLUTIONS
	Yes	**No**	
Drinking Fountains, continued Are controls mounted on the front or on the side near the front edge, and operable with one closed fist?	☐	☐	☐ Replace the controls.
Does the fountain protrude no more than 4 inches into the circulation space?	☐	☐	☐ Place a planter or other cane-detectable barrier on each side at floor level.
Telephones (ADAAG 4.30, 4.31) If pay or public use phones are provided, is there clear floor space of at least 30 by 48 inches in front of at least one?	☐	☐	☐ Move furnishings. ☐ Replace booth with open station.
Is the highest operable part of the phone no higher than 48 inches (up to 54 inches if a side approach is possible)?	☐	☐	☐ Lower telephone.
Does the phone protrude no more than 4 inches into the circulation space?	☐	☐	☐ Place a cane-detectable barrier on each side at floor level.
Does the phone have push-button controls?	☐	☐	☐ Contact phone company to install push-buttons.
Is the phone hearing aid compatible?	☐	☐	☐ Contact phone company to add an induction coil (T-switch).
Is the phone adapted with volume control?	☐	☐	☐ Contact the phone company to add volume control.
Is the phone with volume control identified with appropriate signage?	☐	☐	☐ Add signage.
Is one of the phones equipped with a text telephone (TT or TDD)?	☐	☐	☐ Install a text telephone. ☐ Have a portable text telephone available.
Is the location of the text telephone identified by accessible signage bearing the International TDD Symbol?	☐	☐	☐ Add signage.

International TDD Symbol:

Preparing a REQUEST FOR PROPOSALS to provide ADA BARRIER IDENTIFICATION SERVICES

This document is designed to assist facility managers in preparing RFP's for facility surveys and reports which will be used in their efforts to comply with the requirements of the Americans with Disabilities Act. It has been prepared for those entities who wish to hire consultants who have more expertise or resources than the hiring entity can reasonably obtain otherwise. By providing the information listed, respondents should be able to adequately estimate the level of effort, the degree of thoroughness and the type of detailed recommendations desired in the final report.

Elements of the Request for Proposals

1. Describe the **Purpose** of the study including any key objectives identified by the requesting entity which are beyond ADA requirements.

2. Provide **Background** information for the proposed study such as:

   a. For public entities, state which accessibility standard the entity has adopted for ADA compliance (ADAAG or UFAS).

   b. If the study will review facilities for compliance with any other codes and/or standards, list them.

   c. Describe any prior studies which have been made of the facilities covered by the study and note whether those reports will be made available to the respondents or only to the consultant who is selected.

   d. As an appendix to the RFP, include detailed information about each facility to be surveyed including: primary functions or uses of the facility, square feet of public and employee floor areas to be surveyed, dates that original construction was completed and dates of major modifications. If the study will include employee areas, include any pertinent information about staffing. If available, make site and floor plans available.

3. Detail any requirements for **Coordination** that the consultant will provide to interface this study with the work of any others. This might include, for public entities, self-

evaluations and transition plans. For public or private entities, it might include work needed to comply with the "reasonable accommodations" requirements of Title I.

4. Define the **Scope of work** in terms of the level of detail of the survey (what standard should be used to determine where barriers exist), the thoroughness of the assessment and the types of information and recommendations desired in the final report. If staff training is desired to allow staff to implement the recommendations of the report, implement other requirements of the ADA and to offer other solutions to barriers which might not have been obvious to an outside consultant, describe the training objectives. If assistance with the transition plan and public review and comment requirements of Title II are needed, that should be a part of this scope.*

5. Describe the **Deliverables** needed. Include information about the desired format (if there is a preference), the number of hard copies, any special requirements for digital formats if a database is one of the deliverables and whether or not photographs are required. If staff training is part of the scope, list any special requests for training and reference materials.

6. If **Schedule** is important, give the requirements or preferences.

7. List any pertinent details about **Contracts, fees and payments** that may be a part of the final agreement.

8. If the consultant is expected to incur any **Liability** as a result of the work, describe the expectations or ask for their standard terms of agreement.

9. Review **RFP Logistics** such as how questions will be answered prior to submittal and how the evaluation and selection process will proceed. Include, if applicable, the selection criteria.

10. **Appendix** (facility data)

---

* Other consulting services may be needed to complete the compliance process, however, their scope cannot usually be defined until the survey and report have been analyzed. They may include cost estimating the removal of physical barriers, design and construction documents for some of the barrier removal efforts, review of new construction and alteration projects in progress or tracking expenditures in alterations projects for use in determining the disproportionate limits for future alterations.

Bibliography

Accessibility in Georgia: A Technical and Policy Guide to Access in Georgia, Georgia Division of Rehabilitation Services, 1986.

Adaptable Housing: A Technical Manual for Implementing Adaptable Dwelling Unit Specifications, U.S. Government Printing Office, 1989.

The Americans with Disabilities Act: A Comprehensive Guide to Title I, Society for Human Resource Management, 1992.

The Americans with Disabilities Act: A Practical & Legal Guide to Impact, Enforcement & Compliance, BNA Books, 1990.

Barrier Free Environments, Inc., *Accessible Housing Design File*, Van Nostrand Reinhold, 1991. New York.

Barrier Free Environments, Inc., *UFAS Retrofit Manual*, U.S. Architectural and Transportation Barriers Compliance Board, 1991.

Davies, Thomas, *Design for Hospitality*, Nichols Publishing, 1988.

The Design of Accessible HUD 202 Small Group Homes, Barrier Free Environments, Inc., 1991.

Duston, Robert L., *The Americans with Disabilities Act (ADA) Compliance Manual: A Practical Guide for Mass Retailers*, Schmeltzer, Aptaker & Shepard, 1991.

E.C.H.O. Housing: Recommended Construction and Installation Standards, American Association of Retired Persons, 1984.

Evan Terry Associates, Inc., *Americans with Disabilities Act Facilities Compliance Workbook*, John Wiley & Sons, Inc., 1992.

Goltsman, Susan M., Timothy A. Gilbert, and Steven D. Wohlford, *The Accessibility Checklist: An Evaluation System for Buildings & Outdoor Settings*, MIG Communications, 1992.

The Guide: Facilities Evaluation and Modification Guide, Barrier Free Environments, Inc., 1984.

Bibliography

Laslett, Betty, *The Arts and 504: A 504 Handbook for Accessible Arts Programming*, U.S. Government Printing Office, 1985.

Leibrock, Cynthia A., *Beautiful Barrier Free: A Visual Guide To Accessibility*, Van Nostrand Reinhold, 1992.

Mobile Homes: Alternative Housing for The Handicapped, Barrier Free Environments, Inc., 1976.

Montuori, Don, ed., *Americans with Disabilities Act: ADA Compliance Guide,* Thompson Publishing Group, Inc., 1990.

Moore, Robin, *Play for All Guidelines*, MIG Communications, 1987.

Mueller, James, *The Workplace Workbook: An Illustrated Guide to Job Accommodation and Assistive Technology*, The Dole Foundation. 1990.

Perritt, Henry H., *Americans with Disabilities Act Handbook*, John Wiley & Sons, Inc., 1991.

Pimentel, Richard, *The Americans with Disabilities Act: Making the ADA Work for You, Second Edition*, Society for Human Resource Management, 1992.

The Planner's Guide to Barrier Free Meeting, Barrier Free Environments, Inc., 1980.

Readily Achievable Checklist: A Survey for Accessibility, National Center for Access Unlimited, 1991.

Tysse, G. John, ed., *The Legislative History of the Americans with Disabilities Act*, LRP Publications, 1991.

What Managers and Supervisors Need to Know About the ADA, Society for Human Resource Management, 1992.

Index

Page numbers appearing in *italic* indicate illustrations.

Index